PENGU
SPANISH PH

OTHER PENGUIN PHRASE BOOKS
Dutch
French
German
Greek
Italian
Portuguese
Russian
Turkish

SPANISH
PHRASE BOOK

THIRD EDITION

JILL NORMAN

MARIA VICTORIA ALVAREZ

PEPA ROMAN DE OLINS

PENGUIN BOOKS

PENGUIN BOOKS

Published by the Penguin Group
Penguin Books Ltd, 27 Wrights Lane, London W8 5TZ, England
Viking Penguin, a division of Penguin Books USA Inc.
375 Hudson Street, New York, New York 10014, USA
Penguin Books Australia Ltd, Ringwood, Victoria, Australia
Penguin Books Canada Ltd, 2801 John Street, Markham, Ontario, Canada L3R 1B4
Penguin Books (NZ) Ltd, 182–190 Wairau Road, Auckland 10, New Zealand

Penguin Books Ltd, Registered Offices: Harmondsworth, Middlesex, England

First published in 1968
Second edition 1978
Third edition 1988
7 9 10 8 6

Printed in England by Clays Ltd, St Ives plc
Filmset in Linotron 202 Ehrhardt

CONTENTS

SHOPPING & SERVICES ▪ 110

POST OFFICE ▪ 141

SIGHTSEEING ▪ 146

ENTERTAINMENT ▪ 153

SPORTS & GAMES ▪ 156

ON THE BEACH ▪ 162

IN THE COUNTRY ▪ 166

TRAVELLING WITH CHILDREN ▪ 168

BUSINESS MATTERS ▪ 172

AT THE DOCTOR'S ▪ 174

AT THE DENTIST'S ▪ 184

PROBLEMS & ACCIDENTS ▪ 186

TIME & DATES ▪ 189

INTRODUCTION

To the Third Edition

In this series of phrase books only those words and phrases that might be called essential to a traveller have been included, but the definition of 'traveller' has been made very wide, to include not only the business traveller and the holiday-maker, whether travelling alone, with a group or the family, but also the owner of a house, an apartment or a time-share. Each type of traveller has his or her own requirements, and for easy use the phrases are arranged in sections which deal with specific situations.

Pronunciation is given for each phrase and for all words in the extensive vocabulary. An explanation of the system used for the pronunciation guide is to be found on pages xiii–xv. It is essential to read this section carefully before starting to use this book.

Some of the Spanish phrases are marked with an asterisk* – these give an indication of the kind of reply you might get to your question, and of questions you may be asked in your turn.

For those who would like to know a little more about the Spanish language, a brief survey of the main points of its grammar is provided at the end of the book (pages 202–209).

PRONUNCIATION

The pronunciation guide is intended for people with no knowledge of Spanish. As far as possible the system is based on English pronunciation. This means that complete accuracy may sometimes be lost for the sake of simplicity, but the reader should be able to understand Spanish pronunciation, and make himself understood, if he reads this section carefully. In addition, each word in the vocabulary is given with a pronunciation guide.

VOWELS

All Spanish vowel sounds are pure, they are not slurred as in English. Final **e** is always pronounced.

Pronounce:	**a** as **a** in father	e.g. casa – house (ka-sa)	Symbol **a**
	e as **e** in bed	e.g. negro – black (ne-gro)	Symbol **e**
and	as **ai** in air	e.g. poder – to be able (po-dair)	Symbol **ai, ay**
	i as **i** in machine	e.g. fin – end (feen)	Symbol **ee**
	o as **o** in porter	e.g. todo – all (to-do)	Symbol **o**
	u as **oo** in boot	e.g. mucho – much (moo-cho)	Symbol **oo**

COMPOUND VOWELS

In the groups ia, ie, io the **i** sound resembles y in yes   Symbol **y, ee**
     e.g. alguien – anyone (alg-yen)
In the groups ue, ui, uo the **u** sound resembles w as in wet   Symbol **w, oo**
     e.g. bueno – good (bwe-no)

CONSONANTS

Many are similar to English consonants but note the following:

c before e or i is pronounced **th** as in thin   Symbol **th**
     e.g. cerrar – to shut (ther-rar)
c before a, o, u or a consonant is pronounced **k**   Symbol **k**
     e.g. coche – car (ko-che)
final **d** is not always pronounced
     e.g. edad – age (ay-da)
g before e or i is pronounced like English **h** (hot)   Symbol **h**
    or Scottish **ch** (loch)
     e.g. gente – people (hen-te)
g before a, o, u or a consonant is pronounced **g** as   Symbol **g**
    in got
     e.g. gafas – glasses (ga-fas)
h is always silent
j is like English **h** (hot) or Scottish **ch** (loch)   Symbol **h**
     e.g. mujer – woman (moo-hair)
ll is like **lli** in million   Symbol **lly**
     e.g. llamar – to call (llya-mar)
ñ is like **ni** in onion   Symbol **ny**
     e.g. mañana – morning (ma-nya-na)
q(u) is pronounced as **k**   Symbol **k**
     e.g. queso – cheese (ke-so)

r is trilled, **rr** trilled even more strongly

v is pronounced as **b**   Symbol **b**
    e.g. vaso – glass (ba-so)

z is pronounced **th** as in thin   Symbol **th**
    e.g. manzana – apple (man-tha-na)

This is the pronunciation used in Spain. In Spanish America there are one or two differences, notably **c** + **e** or **i** and **z** are pronounced **s** not **th**.

STRESS

Words ending in a vowel, **n** or **s** are stressed on the last syllable but one: **casa, gafas, venden**.

    Words ending in a consonant other than **n̄** or **s** are stressed on the last syllable: ha**blar**, espa**ñol**.

    Exceptions to these rules are indicated by a written accent: café, autobús, estación. In the pronunciation guide, words with irregular stress have the stressed syllable printed in **bold** type.

ESSENTIALS

FIRST THINGS

Yes	**Sí**	See
No	**No**	No
Please	**Por favor**	Por fabor
Thank you	**Gracias**	Gra-thee-as
You're welcome	**De nada**	De na-da

LANGUAGE PROBLEMS

| I'm English/American | **Soy inglés/americano (inglesa/americana)** | Soy een-**gles**/a-mer-ee-ka-no (een-gle-sa/a-mer-ee-ka-na) |
| Do you speak English? | **¿Habla inglés?** | Ab-la een-**gles** |

Does anyone here speak English?	**¿Habla inglés alguien aquí?**	Ab-la een-**gles** alg-yen a-**kee**
I don't speak Spanish	**No hablo español**	No ab-lo es-pan-yol
I speak a little Spanish	**Hablo un poco español**	Ab-lo oon po-ko es-pan-yol
I understand	**Yo entiendo**	Yo en-tee-en-do
Do you understand (me)?	**¿(Me) entiende?**	(Me) en-tee-end-de
I don't understand	**No entiendo**	No en-tee-en-do
Would you say that again, please?	**Repita eso, por favor**	Re-pee-ta eso por fa-bor
Please speak slowly	**Hable despacio, por favor**	Ab-le des-pa-thee-o por fa-bor
What is it called in Spanish?	**¿Cómo se llama en español?**	Ko-mo se llya-ma en es-pan-yol
How do you say that in Spanish?	**¿Cómo se dice en español?**	Ko-mo se dee-the en es-pan-yol
What does that mean?	**¿Qué significa eso?**	Ke seeg-nee-fee-ka eso
Can you translate this for me?	**¿Puede traducirme esto?**	Pwe-de tra-doo-theer-me es-to
Please write it down	**Por favor escríbamelo**	Por fa-bor es-**kree**-ba-me-lo
Please show me the word in the book	**Por favor enséñeme la palabra en el libro**	Por fa-bor en-**se**-nye-me la pa-la-bra en el lee-bro

QUESTIONS

Where is/are ...?	¿Dónde está/están ...?	Don-de es-ta/es-tan
When?	¿Cuándo?	Kwan-do
Who?	¿Quién?	Kee-en
Why?	¿Por qué?	Por ke
What?	¿Qué?	Ke
How?	¿Cómo?	Ko-mo
How much/many?	¿Cuánto/Cuántos?	Kwan-to/Kwan-tos
How much is/are ...?	¿Cuánto es/son ...?	Kwan-to es/son
How long?	¿Cómo es de largo?	Ko-mo es de lar-go
How far?	¿Qué distancia hay?	Ke dees-tan-thee-a eye
What's that?	¿Qué es eso?	Ke es eso
What do you want?	¿Qué desea?	Ke de-se-a
What must I do?	¿Qué debo hacer?	Ke de-bo a-thair
Have you ...?	¿Tiene ...?	Tee-e-ne
Is/Are there ...?	¿Hay ...?	Eye
Have you seen ...?	¿Ha visto ...?	A bees-to
Where can I find?	¿Dónde puedo encontrar?	Don-de pwe-do en-kon-trar
What is the matter?	¿Qué pasa?	Ke pa-sa
Can you help me?	¿Puede ayudarme?	Pwe-de a-yoo-dar-me
Can I help you?	¿*Puedo ayudarle?	Pwe-do a-yoo-dar-le
Can you tell me/give me/show me?	¿Puede decirme/darme/enseñarme?	Pwe-de de-theer-me/dar-me/en-se-nyar-me

USEFUL STATEMENTS

It is ...	**Sí es ...**	See es
It isn't ...	**No es ...**	No es
I have ...	**Tengo ...**	Ten-go
I don't have ...	**No tengo ...**	No ten-go
I want ...	**Quiero ...**	Kee-e-ro
I would like ...	**Me gustaría ...**	Me goos-ta-**ree**-a
I need ...	**Necesito ...**	Ne-the-see-to
I like it	**Me gusta**	Me goos-ta
OK/That's fine	**Vale/Está bien**	Ba-le/Es-**ta** bee-en
I'm lost	**Estoy perdido**	Es-toy pair-dee-do
We're looking for ...	**Estamos buscando ...**	Es-ta-mos boos-kan-do
Here it is	**Aquí está**	A-kee es-ta
There they are	**Allí están**	A-llyee es-**tan**
There is/are ...	**Hay ...**	Eye
It's important	**Es importante**	Es eem-por-tan-te
It's urgent	**Es urgente**	Es oor-hen-te
You are mistaken	**Está equivocado**	Es-**ta** e-kee-bo-ka-do
I'm not sure	**No estoy seguro**	No es-toy se-goo-ro
I don't know	**No sé**	No se
I didn't know	**No sabía**	No sa-**bee**-a
I think so	**Creo que sí**	Kre-o ke see
I'm hungry/thirsty	**Tengo hambre/sed**	Ten-go am-bre/sed
I'm tired	**Estoy cansado**	Es-toy kan-sa-do
I'm in a hurry	**Tengo prisa**	Ten-go pree-sa

I'm ready	**Estoy listo**	Es-toy lees-to
Leave me alone	**Por favor déjeme**	Por fa-bor **de**-he-me
Just a moment	**Un momento**	Oon mo-men-to
This way, please	**Por aquí sígame**	Por a-**kee** see-ga-me
Take a seat	**Siéntese**	See-**en**-te-se
Come in!	**¡Adelante!**	A-de-lan-te
It's cheap/expensive	**Es barato/caro**	Es ba-ra-to/ka-ro
It's too much	**Es demasiado**	Es de-ma-see-a-do
That's all	**Es todo**	Es to-do
You're right	**Tiene razón**	Tee-e-ne ra-**thon**
You're wrong	**No tiene razón**	No tee-e-ne ra-**thon**
Thank you for your help	**Muchas gracias por su ayuda**	Moo-chas gra-thee-as por soo a-yoo-da
It's beautiful	**Es bonito/precioso**	Es bo-nee-to/pre-thee-o-so

GREETINGS

Good morning/good day	**Buenos días**	Bwe-nos **dee**-as
Good afternoon	**Buenas tardes**	Bwe-nas tar-des
Good evening/good night	**Buenas noches**	Bwe-nas no-ches
Good-bye	**Adiós**	A-dee-os
Hello	**¡Hola!/¿Qué hay?**	O-la/ke eye
How are you?	**¿Cómo está (usted)?**	Ko-mo es-ta (oos-te)
Very well, thank you	**Muy bien, gracias**	Mwee bee-en gra-thee-as

See you soon	**Hasta luego**	As-ta lwe-go
Have a good journey	**¡Buen viaje!**	Bwen bee-a-he
Good luck/all the best	**¡Buena suerte!**	Bwe-na soo-er-te

POLITE PHRASES

Sorry/excuse me	**Perdone**	Pair-do-ne
Excuse me (*to pass*)	**Me permite, por favor**	Me pair-mee-te por fa-bor
That's all right	**Está bien**	Es-ta bee-en
Is everything all right?	**¿Todo bien?**	To-do bee-en
Not at all/don't mention it	**De nada**	De na-da
Don't worry	**No se preocupe**	No se pre-o-koo-pe
It doesn't matter	**No importa**	No eem-por-ta
I beg your pardon?	**¿Qué/¿cómo dice?**	Ke/ko-mo dee-the
Am I disturbing you?	**¿(Le) molesto?**	(Le) mo-les-to
I'm sorry to have troubled you	**Siento haberle molestado**	See-en-to a-bair-le mo-les-ta-do
Good/that's fine	**Bien/está muy bien**	Bee-en/es-ta mwee bee-en
With pleasure	**Con mucho gusto**	Kon moo-cho goos-to

OPPOSITES

before/after	**antes/después**	an-tes/des-**pwes**
early/late	**temprano/tarde**	tem-pra-no/tar-de
first/last	**primero/último**	pree-me-ro/**ool**-tee-mo
now/then	**ahora/entonces**	a-or-a/en-ton-thes
far/near	**lejos/cerca**	le-hos/thair-ka
here/there	**aquí/allí**	a-kee/a-ye
in/out	**en/fuera**	en/fwair-a
inside/outside	**adentro/fuera**	a-den-tro/fwair-a
under/over	**debajo/sobre**	de-ba-ho/so-bre
big, large/small	**grande/pequeño**	gran-de/pe-ken-yo
deep/shallow	**profundo/poco**	pro-foon-do/po-co
empty/full	**vacío/lleno**	ba-**thee**-oh/llye-no
fat/thin	**gordo/fino**	gor-do/fee-no
heavy/light	**pesado/ligero**	pe-sa-doh/lee-hair-o
high/low	**alto/bajo**	al-to/ba-ho
long, tall/short	**largo, alto/corto**	lar-go, al-to/kor-to
narrow/wide	**estrecho/ancho**	es-tre-cho/an-cho
many/few	**muchos/pocos**	moo-chos/po-kos
more/less	**más/menos**	mas/me-nos
much/little	**mucho/poco**	moo-cho/po-ko
beautiful/ugly	**bonito/feo**	bo-nee-to/fay-o
better/worse	**mejor/peor**	me-hor/pe-or
cheap/expensive	**barato/caro**	ba-ra-to/ca-ro

clean/dirty	**limpio/sucio**	leem-pyo/soo-thyo
cold/hot, warm	**frío/caliente**	free-o/ka-lee-en-te
easy/difficult	**fácil/difícil**	fa-theel/dee-**fee**-theel
fresh/stale	**fresco/pasado**	fres-ko/pa-sa-do
good/bad	**bueno/malo**	bwe-no/ma-lo
young/old	**joven/viejo**	ho-ben/bye-ho
new/old	**nuevo/viejo**	nwe-bo/bye-ho
right/wrong	**correcto/incorrecto**	ko-rek-to/een-ko-rek-to
vacant/occupied	**libre/ocupado**	lee-bre/o-koo-pa-do
open/closed, shut	**abierto/cerrado**	a byer-to/ther-ra-do
quick/slow	**rápido/lento**	ra-pee-dol/len-go
quiet/noisy	**tranquilo/ruidoso**	tran-kee-lo/rwee-do-so

SIGNS & PUBLIC NOTICES[1]

Abierto de ... a ...	Open from ... to ...
Agua potable	Drinking water
Ascensor	Life/elevator
Banco	Bank
Caballeros	Gentlemen
Caja	Cash desk
Cerrado	Closed
Circulen por la derecha	Keep right
Comisaría	Police station
Correos	Post office
Empujar	Push
Entrada	Entrance
Entrada gratuita/libre	Admission free
Guía	Guide

1. See also ROAD SIGNS (p. 38).

Hay habitaciones	Vacancies/rooms to let
(Hotel) completo	No vacancies
Información	Information
Intérprete	Interpreter
Lavabos	Lavatory
Libre	Vacant/free/unoccupied
Liquidación	Sale
Llamar	Knock/ring
No hay entradas/localidades	House full (*cinema, etc.*)
No pasar	No entry
No pisar por la hierba	Keep off the grass
No tocar	Do not touch
Ocupado	Engaged/occupied
Particular/privado	Private
Peatones	Pedestrians
Peligro	Danger
Precaución	Caution
Prohibido ... bajo multa de...	Trespassers will be prosecuted
Prohibido el paso	No entry
Reservado	Reserved
Retretes	Lavatory
Saldo	Sale
Salida	Exit
Salida de emergencia	Emergency exit
Se alquila	To let/for hire

Se alquilan habitaciones/ apartamentos	Rooms/flats to let
Señoras	Ladies
Señores	Gentlemen
Se prohibe fumar	No smoking
Se ruega no ...	You are requested not to ...
Servicios	Lavatory
Se vende	For sale
Tirar	Pull

ABBREVIATIONS

a/c	al cuidado de	care of
a. de J.C.	antes de Jesucristo	BC
Avda.	avenida	avenue
C/	calle	street
c/c	cuenta corriente	current account
cía	compañía	company
d. de J.C.	después de Jesucristo	AD
EE UU	Estados Unidos	USA
d., dcha.	derecha	right
f.e.	ferrocarril	railway
h	hora	hour
izq.	izquierda	left
Na. Sra.	Nuestra Señora	Our Lady
No, núm.	número	number

p. ej.	**por ejemplo**	for example
pág.	**página**	page
pta.	**peseta**	peseta
P.V.P.	**precio venta al público**	sale price to the public
R.E.N.F.E.	**Red nacional de ferrocarriles españoles**	Spanish railways
S., Sta.	**san, santa**	saint
S.A.	**sociedad anónima**	ltd, inc.
Sr.	**señor**	Mr
Sra.	**señora**	Mrs
Srta.	**señorita**	Miss
V, Ud.	**usted**	you

MONEY

Exchange	**Cambio**	Kam-bee-o
Is there a bank that changes money near here?	**¿Hay algún banco cerca donde se pueda cambiar dinero?**	Eye al-**goon** ban-ko thair-ka don-de se pwe-da kam-bee-ar dee-ne-ro
Do you cash travellers' cheques?	**¿Cambian cheques de viajero?**	Kam-byan che-kes de bya-**hair**-o
Where can I cash travellers' cheques?	**¿Dónde puedo cambiar cheques de viajero?**	Don-de pwe-do kam-bee-ar che-kes de bya-hair-o
I want to change some English/American money	**Quiero cambiar dinero inglés/americano**	Kee-e-ro kam-bee-ar dee-ne-ro een-**gles**/amer-ee-ka-no
How much do I get for a pound/dollar?	**¿A cuánto está la libra/el dólar?**	A kwan-to es-**ta** la lee-bra/el **dol**-ar
What is the rate of exchange?	**¿A cuánto está el cambio?**	A kwan-to es-**ta** el kam-bee-o
Can you give me some small change?	**Déme algo de dinero suelto, por favor**	**De**-me al-go de dee-ne-ro swel-to por fa-bor

Please cash this Eurocheque	**Por favor cóbreme este cheque**	Por fa-bor **ko**-bre-me es-te che-ke
Will you take a personal cheque?	**¿Aceptan cheques?**	A-thep-tan che-kes
Do you have identification?	***¿Tiene algo que le identifique?**	Tee-e-ne al-go ke le ee-den-tee-fee-ke
Do you have a cheque card?	***¿Tiene una tarjeta de banco?**	Tee-e-ne oon-a tar-he-ta de ban-ko
Will you take a credit card?	**¿Aceptan tarjeta de crédito?**	A-thep-tan tar-het-a de **kre**-dee-to
Where do I sign?	**¿Dónde firmo?**	Don-de feer-mo
Sign here, please	***Firme aquí, por favor**	Feer-me a-**kee** por fa-bor
Go to the cashier	***Vaya a la caja**	Ba-ya a la ka-ha
I arranged for money to be transferred from England, has it arrived yet?	**He hecho una transferencia desde inglaterra ¿ha llegado ya?**	E e-cho oon-a trans-fe-**rain**-thee-a des-de een-gla-tair-ra a llye-ga-do ya
I want to open a bank account	**Quiero abrir una cuenta**	Kee-e-ro a-breer oon-a kwen-ta
Please credit this to my account	**Por favor ponga esto en mi cuenta**	Por fa-bor pon-ga es-to en mee kwen-ta
I'd like to get some cash with my credit card	**Quiero sacar dinero con la tarjeta de crédito**	Kee-er-o sa-kar dee-ne-ro kon la tar-he-ta de **kre**-dee-to
current account	**la cuenta corriente**	kwen-ta kor-ree-en-te
deposit account	**la cuenta depósito**	kwen-ta de-**po**-see-to
statement	**el estadillo de cuentas**	es-ta-dee-llyo de kwen-tas
balance	**el balance**	ba-lan-the

| cheque book | **la talonera de cheques** | ta-lo-ne-ra de che-kes |
| cheque card | **la tarjeta de banco** | tar-he-ta de ban-ko |

CURRENCY

Spanish currency is the peseta. A 5-peseta coin is commonly called a **duro**, and prices are sometimes quoted as so many **duros**, e.g. 20 **duros** means 100 pesetas.

TRAVEL

ARRIVAL

PASSPORTS

Passport control	*Control de pasaportes	Kon-trol de pasa-por-tes
Your passport, please	*El pasaporte, por favor	El pasa-por-te por fa-bor
May I see your green card?	*¿Me permite ver su tarjeta verde?	Me pair-mee-te bair soo tar-he-ta bair-de
Are you together?	*¿Viajan juntos?	Bya-han hoon-tos
I'm travelling alone	Viajo solo	Bya-ho so-lo
I'm travelling with my wife/a friend	Viajo con mi esposa/un amigo	Bya-ho kon mee es-po-sa/oon a-mee-go
I'm here on business/ on holiday	Vengo de negocios/ de vacaciones	Ben-go de nego-thyos/de ba-ka-thyo-nes

| What is your address in Madrid? | *¿(Cuál es) su dirección en Madrid? | (Kwal es) soo dee-rek-thyon en Ma-drid |
| How long are you staying here? | *¿Cuánto tiempo va a estar usted aquí? | Kwan-to tee-em-po ba a es-tar oos-te a-kee |

CUSTOMS

Customs	*Aduana	A-dwan-a
Goods to declare	*Artículos que declarar	Ar-tee-koo-loos ke de-kla-rar
Nothing to declare	*Nada que declarar	Na-da ke de-kla-rar
Which is your luggage?	*¿Cuál es su equipaje?	Kwal es soo e-kee-pa-he
Do you have more luggage?	*¿Tiene más equipaje?	Tee-e-ne mas e-kee-pa-he
This is (all) my luggage	Esto es (todo) mi equipaje	Es-to es (to-do) mee e-kee-pa-he
Have you anything to declare?	*¿Tiene algo que declarar?	Tee-e-ne al-go ke de-kla-rar
I have only my personal things in it	Sólo llevo mis cosas personales	So-lo llye-bo mees ko-sas pair-son-al-es
I have a carton of cigarettes and a bottle of brandy/wine	Llevo un cartón de tabaco y una botella de coñac/vino	Llye-bo oon kar-ton de ta-ba-ko ee oon-a bo-te-llya de kon-yak/bi-no
You will have to pay duty on this	*Esto paga aduana	Es-to pa-ga a-dwan-a
Open your bag please	*Abra la maleta, por favor	Ab-ra la ma-le-ta por fa-bor

Can I shut my case now?	¿Puedo cerrar la maleta ya?	Pwe-do the-rar la ma-le-ta ya
May I go through?	¿Puedo pasar ya?/ ¿puedo irme?	Pwe-do pa-sar ya/pwe-do eer-me

LUGGAGE

Where is the information bureau, please?	¿Dónde está la oficina de Información?	Don-de es-ta la o-fee-thee-na de een-for-ma-thyon
My luggage has not arrived	Mi equipaje no ha llegado	Mee e-kee-pa-he no a llye-ga-do
My luggage is damaged	Mi equipaje está dañado	Mee e-kee-pa-he es-ta da-nya-do
One suitcase is missing	Falta una maleta/un bulto	Falta oon-a ma-le-ta/oon bool-to
Are there any luggage trolleys?	¿Hay carritos para el equipaje?	Eye kar-ree-tos pa-ra el e-kee-pa-he
Where is the left luggage office?	¿Dónde está la consigna?	Don-de es-ta la kon-seeg-na
Luggage lockers	Consigna automática	Kon-seeg-na ow-to-ma-tee-ka

MOVING ON

Porter	Mozo	Mo-tho
Would you take these bags to a taxi/the bus	Lléveme estas maletas a un taxi/ al autobús	Llye-be-me es-tas ma-le-tas a oon taxi/al ow-toh-**boos**

What's the price for each piece of luggage?	**¿Cuánto cuesta cada bulto?**	Kwan-to kwes-ta ka-da bool-to
I shall take this myself	**Yo llevo esto**	Yo llye-bo es-to
That's not mine	**Eso no es mío**	Eso no es mee-o
How much do I owe?	**¿Cuánto le debo?**	Kwan-to le de-bo
Is there a bus/train into the town?	**¿Hay tren o autobús a la ciudad?**	Eye tren o ow-toh-**boos** a la thee-oo-dad
How can I get to ...?	**¿Cómo puedo llegar a ...?**	Ko-mo pwe-do llye-gar a ...

SIGNS TO LOOK FOR AT AIRPORTS AND STATIONS

Arrivals	**Llegadas**
Booking office	**Despacho de billetes/taquilla**
Buses	**Autobuses**
Car rental	**Alquiler de coches**
Connections	**Combinación**
Departures	**Salidas**
Exchange	**Cambio**
Gentlemen	**Servicios/caballeros/señores**
Hotel reservations	**Reservas hotel**
Information	**Información**
Ladies	**Servicios/señoras**
Left luggage	**Consigna**
Lost property	**Oficina de objetos perdidos**

Luggage lockers	**Consigna automática**
Newsstand	**Kiosco**
No smoking	**Se prohibe fumar**
Refreshments[1]	**Cafetería/fonda/bar/restaurante**
Reservations	**Reservas**
Suburban lines	**Trenes de cercanías/trenes cortos**
Taxi rank	**Parada de taxis**
Tickets	**Billetes**
Transit desk	**Mostrador de tránsito**
Tourist office	**Oficina de turismo**
Underground	**Metro**
Waiting room	**Sala de espera**

BUYING A TICKET[2]

Where is the nearest travel agency?	**¿Dónde está la agencia de viajes más próxima?**	Don-de es-ta la a-hen-thee-a de bya-hes mas pro-see-ma
Have you a timetable, please?	**¿Tiene(n) un horario?**	Tee-e-ne(n) oon or-a-ree-o

1. In a station the **cafetería** serves drinks and snacks; the **fonda** also serves meals and lets rooms.
2. La RENFE, the Spanish railway system, has an office in the centre of most large towns. As ticket offices at railway stations only issue tickets shortly before the departure of the train most people book their tickets and reserve seats in advance at the RENFE office. You can buy a ticket called a **kilométrico** if you intend to travel long distances in Spain.

A ticket to ...	**Un billete para ...**	Oon bee-llye-te pa-ra
How much is it first class to ...?	**¿Cuánto cuesta un billete de primera a ...?**	Kwan-to kwes-ta oon bee-llye-te de pree-mair-a a
A second class to ...	**Un billete de segunda a ...**	Oon bee-llye-te de se-goon-da a
A single/one way to ...	**Un billete de ida a ...**	Oon bee-llye-te de ee-da a
A (day) return to ...	**Un billete de ida y vuelta (en el día) a ...**	Oon bee-llye-te de ee-da ee bwel-ta (en el **dee**-a) a
How long is this ticket valid?	**¿Cuánto tiempo dura este billete?**	Kwan-to tee-em-po doo-ra es-te bee-llye-te
Is there a cheaper midweek/weekend fare?	**¿Hay precio especial de mitad de semana/fin de semana?**	Eye pre-thyo es-pe-thyal de mee-tad de se-ma-na/feen de se-ma-na
When are you coming back?	**¿Cuándo vuelve?**	Kwan-do bwel-be
A book of tickets[1]	**Un taco (de billetes)**	Oon ta-ko (de bee-llye-tes)
Can I use it on the bus and the underground?	**¿Puedo utilizarlo en el autobús y metro también?**	Pwe-do oo-tee-lee-thar-lo en el ow-toh-**boos** ee me-tro tam-**byen**
Is there a supplementary charge?	**¿Hay que pagar algún suplemento?**	Eye ke pa-gar al-**goon** soo-ple-men-to

---

1. This is only available for underground journeys.

| Is there a special rate for children? | ¿Hay un precio especial para niños? | Eye oon pre-thyo es-pe-thyal pa-ra nee-nyos |
| How old is he/she? | *¿Qué edad tiene el niño? | Ke e-dad tee-e-ne el nee-nyo |

BY TRAIN[1]

RESERVATIONS AND INQUIRIES

Where's the railway station?	¿Dónde está la estación de ferrocarril?	Don-de es-ta la es-ta-thyon de fer-ro-kar-ril
Where is the ticket office?	¿Dónde está la taquilla/la oficina de billetes?	Don-de es-ta la ta-kee-llya/la o-fee-thee-na de bee-llye-tes
Two seats on the train tomorrow to ...	Dos reservas para mañana en el tren de ...	Dos re-sair-bas pa-ra ma-nya-na en el tren de ...
I want	Quiero	Kee-e-ro
a window seat	un asiento con ventana	oon a-see-en-to kon ben-ta-na
a corner seat	un asiento en la esquina	oon a-see-en-to en la es-kee-na
a seat in a smoking compartment	un asiento en el departamento de fumadores	oon a-see-en-to en el de-par-ta-men-to de foo-ma-do-res

1. For help in understanding these and similar questions see TIME & DATES (p. 189), NUMBERS (p. 195Z), DIRECTIONS (p. 33).

I want to reserve a sleeper	**Quiero reservar una litera**	Kee-e-ro re-sair-bar oon-a lee-tair-a
I want to register this luggage through to ...	**Quiero facturar este equipaje directamente a ...**	Kee-e-ro fak-too-rar es-te e-kee-pa-he dee-rek-ta-men-te a ...
When is the next train to ...?	**¿Cuándo sale el próximo tren para ...?**	Kwan-do sa-le el pro-see-mo tren pa-ra
What sort of train is it?[1]	**¿Qué clase de tren es?**	Ke kla-se de tren es
Is there an earlier/later train?	**¿Hay un tren antes de/más tarde de ...?**	Eye oon tren an-tes de/ mas tar-de de
Is there a restaurant car on the train?	**¿Lleva restaurante el tren?**	Llye-ba res-tow-ran-te el tren
I'd like to make a motorail reservation	**Quiero hacer una reserva en el coche-tren**	Kee-e-ro a-thair oon-a re-sair-ba en el ko-che tren
Where is the motorail loading platform?	**¿Dónde está el andén para el coche-tren?**	Don-de es-ta el an-den pa-ra el ko-che-tren

CHANGING

| Is there a through train to ...? | **¿Hay tren directo a ...?** | Eye tren dee-rek-to a ... |
| Do I have to change? | **¿Hay que hacer transbordo?** | Eye ke a-thair trans-bor-do |

1. The following kinds of train run in Spain: **talgo**, **ter**, and **electro tren**, for which one pays first or second class fare plus a supplement; **rápido** and **expreso** – ordinary trains; **correo** and **autovía** are slow trains. **Autoexpreso** is the car-sleeper express.

Where do I change?	¿Dónde hay que transbordar?	Don-de eye ke trans-bor-dar
When is there a connection to ...?	¿Cuándo hay combinación para ir a ...?	Kwan-do eye kom-bee-na-thyon pa-ra eer a
Change at ... and take the local train	*Cambiar en ... y coger el tren local	Kam-bee-ar en ... ee ko-hair el tren lo-kal

DEPARTURE

When does the train leave?	¿A qué hora sale el tren?	A ke o-ra sa-le el tren
Which platform does the train to ... leave from?	¿De qué andén sale el tren para ...?	De ke an-den sa-le el tren pa-ra
Is this the train for ...?	¿Es éste el tren para ...?	Es es-te el tren pa-ra
There will be a delay of ...	*Habrá un retraso de ...	A-bra oon re-tra-so de ...

ARRIVAL

When does it get to ...?	¿A qué hora llega a ...?	A ke o-ra llye-ga a
Does the train stop at ...?	¿Para el tren en ...?	Pa-ra el tren en
How long do we stop here?	¿Cuánto tiempo paramos aquí?	Kwan-to tee-em-po pa-ra-mos a-kee
Is the train late?	¿Tiene retraso el tren?	Tee-e-ne re-tras-so el tren

| When does the train from ... get in? | ¿A qué hora llega el tren que viene de ...? | A ke o-ra llye-ga el tren ke bee-e-ne de |
| At which platform? | ¿En qué andén? | En ke an-**den** |

ON THE TRAIN

We have reserved seats	**Tenemos reservas**	Ten-e-mos re-sair-bas
Is this seat free?	**¿Está este asiento libre?**	Es-ta es-te a-see-en-to lee-bre
This seat is taken	**Este asiento está ocupado**	Es-te a-see-en-to es-ta o-koo-pa-do
Is this a smoking/ non-smoking compartment?	**¿Este departamento es de fumadores/ no fumadores?**	Es-te de-par-ta-men-to es de foo-ma-do-res/no foo-ma-do-res
Dining car	**Coche-restaurante**	Ko-che res-tow-ran-te
When is the buffet car open?	**¿Cuándo se abre el restaurante?**	Kwan-do se a-bre el res-tow-ran-te
Where is the sleeping car?	**¿Dónde está el coche-cama?**	Don-de es-ta el ko-che ka-ma
Which is my sleeper?	**¿Cuál es mi litera?**	Kwal es mee lee-tair-a
The heating is very high/low	**La calefacción está muy alta/baja**	La ka-le-fa-**thyon** es-ta mwee al-ta/ba-ha
I can't open/close the window	**No puedo abrir/ cerrar la ventana**	No pwe-do a-breer/ther-rar la ben-ta-na
What station is this?	**¿Qué estación es esta?**	Ke es-ta-**thyon** es es-ta

BY AIR

Where's the airline office?	¿Dónde está la oficina de líneas aéreas?	Don-de es-ta la o-fee-thee-na de lee-ne-as eye-re-as
I'd like to book two seats on the plane to...	Quiero reservar dos billetes para el avión de ...	Kee-e-ro re-sair-bar dos bee-llye-tes pa-ra al a-byon de
Is there a flight to ...?	¿Hay algún vuelo a ...?	Eye al-goon bwe-lo a
When does it leave?	¿A qué hora sale el avión?	A ke o-ra sa-le el a-byon
When does it arrive?	¿A qué hora llega?	A ke o-ra llye-ga
When's the next plane?	¿A qué hora es el próximo avión?	A ke o-ra es el pro-see-mo a-byon
Is there a bus/train to the airport/town/ centre?	¿Hay autobús/tren al aeropuerto/a la ciudad/al centro?	Eye ow-toh-boos/tren al eye-ro-pwer-to/a la thee-oo-dad/al then-tro
When must I check in?	¿A qué hora hay que presentarse?	A ke o-ra eye ke pre-sen-tar-se
Please cancel my reservation to ...	Quiero anular mi reserva para ...	Kee-e-ro a-noo-lar me re-sair-ba pa-ra
I'd like to change my reservation to ...	Quiero cambiar mi reserva para ...	Kee-e-ro kam-bee-ar mee re-sair-ba pa-ra
I have an open ticket	Tengo un billete abierto	Ten-go oon bee-llye-te a-bee-air-to
Can I change my ticket?	¿Puedo cambiar mi billete?	Pwe-do kam-bee-ar mee bee-llye-te
Will it cost more?	¿Me costará más?	Me kos-ta-ra mas

| What is the flight number? | ¿Cuál es el número de vuelo? | Kw-al es el **noo**-me-ro de bwe-lo |

BY BOAT

Is there a boat from here to …?	¿Hay barco de aquí a …?	Eye bar-ko de a-**kee** a
How long does the boat take?	¿Cuánto tiempo tarda?	Kwan-to tee-em-po tar-da
How often does the boat leave?	¿Cada cuánto tiempo sale el barco?	Ka-da kwan-to tee-em-po sa-le el bar-ko
Does the boat call at …?	¿Toca (el barco) en …?	To-ka (el bar-ko) en
When does the next boat leave?	¿Cuándo sale el próximo barco?	Kwan-do sa-le el **pro**-see-mo bar-ko
Can I book a single berth cabin?	¿Puedo reservar un camarote individual?	Pwe-do re-sair-bar oon ka-ma-ro-te een-dee-bee-doo-al
a first class cabin?	un camarote de primera?	oon ka-ma-ro-te de pree-mair-a
a second class cabin?	un camarote de segunda?	oon ka-ma-ro-te de se-goon-da
a luxury cabin?	un camarote de lujo?	oon ka-ma-ro-te de loo-ho
How many berths are there in this cabin?	¿Cuántas literas hay en esta cabina?	Kwan-tas lee-tair-as eye en es-ta ka-bee-na
How do we get on to the deck?	¿Cómo podemos subir a cubierta?	Ko-mo po-de-mos soo-beer a koo-byair-ta
When must we go on board?	¿A qué hora hay que estar a bordo?	A ke o-ra eye ke es-tar a bor-do

When do we dock?	¿A qué hora se desembarca?	A ke o-ra se de-sem-bar-ka
How long do we stay in port?	¿Cuánto tiempo estamos en el puerto?	Kwan-to tee-em-po es-ta-mos en el pwer-to
(car) ferry	ferry (de coches)	fair-ree (de ko-ches)
lifebelt	la salvavidas	sal-ba-bee-das
lifeboat	la lancha salvavidas	lan-cha sal-ba-bee-das

BY UNDERGROUND

Where is the nearest underground station?	¿Dónde está la estación de metro más cercana?	Don-de es-ta la es-ta-thyon de me-tro mas thair-ka-na
Which line goes to ...?	¿Qué línea va a ...?	Ke lee-nea ba a
Does this train go to ...?	¿Este tren va a ...?	Es-te tren ba a...
Where do I change for ...?	¿Dónde tengo que cambiar para ...?	Don-de ten-go ke kam-bee-ar pa-ra
Is the next station ...?	¿Es la próxima estación ...?	Es la pro-see-ma es-ta-thyon
What station is this?	¿Qué estación es esta?	Ke es-ta-thyon es es-ta
Have you an underground map?	¿Tiene un mapa del metro?	Tee-e-ne oon ma-pa del me-tro

BY BUS OR COACH[1]

Where's the bus/coach station?	¿Dónde está la estación de autobuses/coches de línea?	Don-de es-ta la es-ta-thyon de ow-toh-boos-es/ko-ches de lee-nea
Bus stop	*Parada de autobuses	Pa-ra-da de ow-toh-boos-es
Request stop	*Parada discrecional	Pa-ra-da dees-kre-thyo-nal
When does the coach leave?	¿A qué hora sale el autocar?	A ke o-ra sa-le el ow-toh-kar
When does the coach get to?	¿A qué hora llega el autocar a …?	A ke o-ra llye-ga el ow-toh-kar a
What stops does it make?	¿En qué sitios para?	En ke see-tee-os pa-ra
How long is the journey?	¿Cuánto se tarda?	Kwan-to se tar-da
We want to take a coach tour round the sights	Queremos visitar los sitios de interés en autocar	Ke-rai-mos bee-see-tar los see-tee-os de een-te-res en ow-toh-kar
Is there a sightseeing tour?	¿Hay un recorrido turístico/una excursión?	Eye oon re-kor-ee-do too-rees-tee-ko/oon-a es-koor-syon
What is the fare?	¿Cuánto cuesta (el billete)?	Kwan-to kwes-ta (el bee-llye-te)

1. La RENFE, the railway company, also runs coaches between certain towns, and tickets can be bought from RENFE offices. Privately owned coaches, known as **coches de línea**, ply mainly between villages.

Does the bus/coach stop at our hotel?	¿El autobús/el autocar para en nuestro hotel?	El ow-toh-**boos**/el ow-toh-kar pa-ra en noo-es-tro o-tel
Is there an excursion to ... tomorrow?	¿Hay alguna excursión a ... mañana?	Eye al-goo-na es-koor-syon a ... ma-nya-na
Does this bus go to the town centre? to the beach? to the station?	¿Va este autobús al centro? a la playa? la estación?	Ba es-te ow-toh-**boos** al then-tro a la pla-ya a la es-ta-**thyon**
When's the next bus?	¿Cuándo sale el próximo autobús?	Kwan-do sa-le el **pro**-see-mo ow-toh-**boos**
How often do the buses run?	¿Cada cuánto tiempo hay autobús?	Ka-da kwan-to tee-em-po eye ow-toh-**boos**
Has the last bus gone?	¿Ha salido ya el último autobús?	A sa-lee-do ya el **ool**-tee-mo ow-toh-**boos**
Does this bus go near ...?	¿Pasa este autobús cerca de ...?	Pa-sa es-te ow-toh-**boos** thair-ka de
Where can I get a bus to ...?	¿Dónde puedo tomar el autobús para ...?	Don-de pwe-do tom-ar el ow-toh-**boos** pa-ra
Which bus goes to ...?	¿Qué autobús va a ...?	Ke ow-toh-**boos** va a
I want to go to ...	Quiero ir a ...	Kee-e-ro eer a
Where do I get off?	¿Dónde tengo que bajarme?	Don-de ten-go ke ba-har-me
The bus to ... stops over there	*El autobús de ... para allí	El ow-toh-**boos** de ... pa-ra a-**llyee**
You must take a number ...	*Tome el ...	To-me el

You get off at the next stop | *Bájese en la próxima parada | Bah-es-se en la pro-see-ma pa-ra-da
The buses run every ten minutes/every hour | *Hay autobuses cada diez minutos/cada hora | Eye ow-toh-boos-es ka-da dy-eth mee-noo-tos/ka-da o-ra

BY TAXI

Please get me a taxi	**Por favor, (llámeme) un taxi**	Por fa-bor (llya-me-me) oon ta-xi
Where can I find a taxi?	**¿Dónde puedo encontrar un taxi?**	Don-de pwe-do en-kon-trar oon ta-xi
Are you free?	**¿Está libre?**	Es-ta lee-bre
Please take me to the Madrid hotel	**Al hotel Madrid por favor**	Al o-tel ma-drid por fa-bor
Please take me to the station	**A la estación por favor**	A la es-ta-thyon por fa-bor
Please take me to this address	**A esta dirección por favor**	A es-ta dee-rek-thyon por fa-bor
Can you hurry, I'm late	**Dése prisa, por favor; llego tarde**	De-se pree-sa por fa-bor llye-go tar-de
Please wait for me here	**Espere aquí, por favor**	Es-pe-re a-kee por fa-bor
Stop here	**Pare aquí**	Pa-re a-kee
Is it far?	**¿Está lejos?**	Es-ta le-hos
How far is it to ...?	**¿Cuánto hay a ...?**	Kwan-to eye a

Turn right/left at the next corner	En la próxima esquina tuerza a la derecha/izquierda	En la pro-see-ma es-kee-na twer-tha a la de-re-cha/eeth-kee-air-da
Straight on	Todo recto	To-do rek-to
How much do you charge by the hour/ for the day?	¿Cuánto cobra por hora/todo el día?	Kwan-to ko-bra por o-ra/to-do el dee-a
How much will you charge to take me to ...?	¿Cuánto costaría ir a ...?	Kwan-to kos-ta-ree-a eer a
How much is it?	¿Cuánto es?	Kwan-to es
That's too much	Es demasiado	Es de-ma-see-a-do

DIRECTIONS

Excuse me, could you tell me ...?	¿Perdone, podría usted decirme ...?	Pair-do-ne pod-**ree**-a oos-te de-theer-me
Where is ...?	¿Dónde está ...?	Don-de es-**ta**
How do I get to ...?	¿Por dónde se va a ...?	Por don-de se ba a
How far is it to ...?	¿Qué distancia hay a ...?	Ke dees-**tan**-thee-a eye a
How many kilometres?	¿Cuántos kilómetros?	Kwan-tos kee-**lo**-me-tros
How do we get on to the motorway to ...?	¿Por dónde se sale a la autopista de ...?	Por don-de se sa-le a la ow-to-pees-ta de
Which is the best road to ...?	¿Cuál es la mejor carretera para ...?	Kwa-l es la me-hor kar-re-te-ra pa-ra
Is there a scenic route to ...?	¿Hay una ruta pintoresca a ...?	Eye oon-a roo-ta peen-to-res-ka a
Is this the right road for ...?	¿Es ésta la carretera para ...?	Es es-ta la kar-re-te-ra pa-ra
Where does this road lead to?	¿A dónde va esta carretera?	A don-de ba es-ta kar-re-te-ra

Is it a good road?	¿Es buena la carretera?	Es bwe-na la kar-re-te-ra
Is there a motorway?	¿Hay autopista?	Eye ow-to-pees-ta
Is there a toll?	¿Hay peaje?	Eye pe-a-he
Is the tunnel/pass open?	¿Está abierto el túnel/puerto?	Es-ta a-bee-air-to el too-nel/pwer-to
Is the road to ... clear?	¿La carretera para ... está bien?	La kar-re-tei-ra pa-ra ... es-ta bee-en
How far is the next village/the next petrol station?	¿A qué distancia está el próximo pueblo/la próxima gasolinera?	A ke dees-tan-thee-a es-ta el pro-see-mo pwe-blo/la pro-see-ma ga-so-lee-naira
Will we get to ... by evening?	¿Llegaremos a ... antes de anochecer?	Llye-gar-e-mos a ... an-tes de ano-che-thair
How long will it take by car? by bicycle? by foot?	¿Cuánto se tarda en coche? en bicicleta? a pie?	Kwan-to se tar-da en ko-che en bee-thee-klay-ta a pee-ay
Where are we now?	¿Dónde estamos ahora?	Don-de es-ta-mos a-ora
What is the name of this place?	¿Cuál es el nombre de este sitio?	Kwa-l es el nom-bre de es-te see-tee-o
Please show me on the map	Indíquemelo en el mapa, por favor	Een-dee-ke-me-lo en el ma-pa por fa-bor
It's that way	*Es por ahí	Es por eye-ee
It isn't far	*No está lejos	No es-ta le-hos
Follow signs for ...	*Seguir las señales para ...	Se-geer las se-nya-les pa-ra

Follow this road for 5 kilometres	*Siga esta carretera unos cinco kilómetros	See-ga es-ta kar-re-te-ra oon-os theen-ko kee-lo-me-tros
Keep straight on	*Siga adelante/derecho	See-ga a-del-ante/de-re-cho
Turn right at the crossroads	*Tuerza a la derecha en el cruce	Two-er-tha a la de-re-cha en el kroo-the
Take the second road on the left	*Tome la segunda carretera a la izquierda	To-me la se-goon-da kar-re-te-ra a la eeth-kyair-da
Turn right at the traffic lights	*Tuerza a la derecha en el semáforo	Two-er-tha a la de-re-cha en el se-ma-for-o
Turn left after the bridge	*Tuerza a la izquierda después del puente	Two-er-tha a la eeth-kyair-da des-pwes del pwen-te
The best road is the ...	*La mejor carretera es la ...	La meh-or kar-re-te-ra es la
Take the ... and ask again	*Tome la ... y pregunte de nuevo	To-me la ... ee preg-oon-te de nwe-bo
You are going the wrong way	Va equivocado/dirección contraria	Ba e-kee-bo-ka-do/dee-rek-thyon kon-tra-ree-a
one-way system	dirección única	dee-rek-thyon oo-nee-ka
north	norte	nor-te
south	sur	soor
east	este	es-te
west	oeste	o-es-te

DRIVING

Where is the nearest garage?	¿Dónde está el garaje más próximo?	Don-de es-ta el ga-ra-he mas **pro**-see-mo
How far is the next petrol station?	¿A qué distancia está la próxima gasolinera?	A ke dees-**tan**-thee-a es-ta la **pro**-see-ma ga-so-lee-**nair**-a
Have you a road map?	¿Tiene un mapa de carreteras?	Tee-e-ne oon ma-pa de kar-re-te-ras
Where is there a car park?	¿Dónde hay un aparcamiento?	Don-de eye oon a-par-ka-mee-ento
Can I park here?	¿Puedo aparcar aquí?	Pwe-do a-par-kar a-**kee**
How long can I park here?	¿Por cuánto tiempo puedo aparcar aquí?	Por kwan-to tee-em-po pwe-do a-par-kar a-**kee**
Have you any change for the meter please?	¿Tiene cambio para el parquímetro?	Tee-e-ne kam-byo pa-ra el par-kee-me-tro
May I see your licence/logbook, please?	*¿Su permiso/la documentación del coche, por favor?	Soo pair-mees-o/la do-koo-men-ta-**thyon** del ko-che por fa-bor

Is this your car?	*¿Es este su coche?	Es es-te soo ko-che
speed limit	*límite de velocidad	lee-mee-te de be-lo-thee-dad
pedestrian precinct	*recinto de peatones	re-theen-to de pea-to-nes

CAR HIRE

Where can I hire a car?	¿Dónde puedo alquilar un coche?	Don-de pwe-do al-kee-lar oon ko-che
I want to hire a small/large car	Quiero alquilar un coche pequeño/grande	Kee-e-ro al-kee-lar oon ko-che pe-ke-nyo/gran-de
I want to hire an automatic	Quiero alquilar un coche automático	Kee-e-ro al-kee-lar oon ko-che ow-to-ma-tee-ko
Is there a weekend rate?	¿Hay precio especial de fin de semana?	Eye pre-thyo es-pe-thyal de feen de se-ma-na
Is there a midweek rate?	¿Hay precio especial de mitad de semana?	Eye pre-thyo es-pe-thyal de mee-tad de se-ma-na
How much is it by the hour? by the day? by the week?	¿Cuánto cuesta por hora? por día? por semana?	Kwan-to kwes-ta por o-ra por dee-a por se-ma-na
Does that include mileage?	¿Está incluido el kilometraje?	Es-ta een-kloo-ee-do el kee-lo-me-tra-he
The charge per kilometre is …	*El precio por kilómetro es …	El pre-thyo por kee-lo-met-ro es
Do you want full insurance?	*¿Quiere seguro a todo riesgo?	Kee-e-re se-goo-ro a to-do ree-es-go

May I see your driving licence?	*¿Su permiso de conducir?	Soo per-mee-so de kon-doo-theer
Can I return it to your office in ...?	¿Puedo mandárselo a su oficina de ...?	Pwe-do man-dar-se-lo a soo o-fee-thee-na de
Do you want a deposit?	¿Tengo que dejar una señal?	Ten-go ke de-har oon-a se-nyal
I will pay by credit card	Pagaré con tarjeta de crédito	Pa-ga-re kon tar-he-ta de kre-dee-to
Could you show me how to work the lights? the windscreen wipers? the horn? this?	¿Puede enseñarme a usar las luces? el limpiapara-brisas? el claxon? esto?	Pwe-de en-sen-yar-me a oos-ar las loo-thes el leem-pee-a-pa-ra-bree-sas el klak-son es-to

ROAD SIGNS

Aduana	Customs
Alto	Stop
Aparcamiento	Car park
Atención/Precaución	Caution
Autopista	Motorway
Calle estrecha	Narrow road
Carretera cortada	No through road
Carretera obstruida/cerrada	Road blocked/closed
Carril autobús	Bus lane
Ceda el paso	Give way

Circulen por la derecha	Keep right
Cuidado/Precaución	Caution
Curvas (peligrosas)	(Dangerous) bends
Desnivel	Steep hill
Despacio	Slow
Desprendimiento de rocas	Falling rocks
Desviación	Diversion
Dirección prohibida	No entry
Dirección única/obligatoria	One way street
Encender las luces delanteras	Switch on headlights
Estacionamiento prohibido	No parking
Estacionamiento limitado	Limited parking
Excavaciones	Poor road surface
Hielo	Icy surface
Inundaciones	Flooding
Obras	Roadworks
Paso a nivel	Railway (level) crossing
Peaje	Toll
Peatones	Pedestrians
Peligro	Danger
Prohibido adelantar	No overtaking
Prohibido el paso	No entry
Salido de camiones	Lorry exit
Solo para peatones	Pedestrians only
Zona azul	Limited parking zone
Zona libre de aparcamiento	End of no parking zone

AT THE GARAGE OR PETROL STATION

...litres of standard/ premium petrol please	...litros de normal/ super, por favor	... lee-tros de nor-mal/ soo-per por fa-bor
Fill it up please	Llénelo, por favor	Llye-ne-lo por fa-bor
How much is petrol a litre?	¿A cuánto el litro?	A kwan-to el lee-tro
The oil needs changing	El aceite necesita cambiarse	El a-thay-te ne-the-see-ta kam-bee-ar-se
Please clean the windscreen	Límpieme el parabrisas, por favor	Leem-pee-e-me el para-bree-sas por fa-bor
Please check the battery the brakes the oil the tyre pressure, including the spare	Por favor compruebe la batería los frenos el aceite la presión de los neumáticos, incluido el de recambio	Por fa-bor-com-proo-e-be la ba-tair-ree-a los fre-nos el a-thay-te la pre-syon de los ne-oo-ma-tee-kos een-kloo-ee-do el de re-kam-byo
Please wash the car	Láveme el coche, por favor	La-be-me el ko-che por fa-bor
Can I leave the car here?	¿Puedo dejar aquí el coche?	Pwe-do de-har a-kee el ko-che
What time does the garage close?	¿A qué hora se cierra el garaje?	A ke o-ra se thee-er-ra el ga-ra-he
Where are the toilets?	¿Dónde están los servicios?	Don-de es-tan los sair-bee-thyos

REPAIRS

Can you give me a lift to a telephone?	¿Me puede llevar hasta un teléfono?	Me pwe-de llye-bar as-ta oon te-le-fo-no
Please tell the next garage to send help	¿Por favor puede pedir ayuda en el próximo garaje?	Por fa-bor pwe-de pe-deer a-yoo-da en el pro-see-mo ga-ra-he
Is there a ... agent here?	¿Hay aquí agencia ...?	Eye a-kee a-hen-theea
Have you a breakdown service?	¿Hay servicio de avería?	Eye sair-bee-thyo de a-ber-ee-a
Is there a mechanic?	¿Hay un mecánico?	Eye oon me-ka-nee-ko
May I use your phone?	¿Puedo usar su teléfono?	Pwe-do oos-ar soo-te-le-fo-no
My car's broken down, can you send someone to tow it?	He tenido avería en el coche, ¿puede mandarme una grúa?	E ten-ee-do a-ber-ee-a en el ko-che pwe-de man-dar-me oon-a groo-a
Can you send someone to look at it?	¿Puede enviar a alguien que lo vea?	Pwe-de en-bee-ar a al-gee-en ke lo be-a
It is an automatic and cannot be towed	Es automático y no puede remolcarse	Es ow-to-ma-tee-ko ee no pwe-de re-mol-kar-se
Where are you?	*¿Dónde está usted?	Don-de es-ta oos-te
Where is your car?	*¿Dónde está su coche?	Don-de es-ta soo ko-che
I'm on the road from ... to ..., near kilometre post ...	Estoy en la carretera de ... a ..., cerca del poste del kilómetro ...	Es-toy en la kar-re-te- de ... a ...

How long will you be?	¿Cuánto tiempo tardará?	Kwan-to tee-em-po tar-da-ra
I've lost my car key	He perdido la llave del coche	E per-dee-do la llya-be del ko-che
The battery is flat, it needs charging	La batería está desgastada, necesita cargarse	La ba-tai-ree-a es-ta des-gas-ta-da ne-the-see-ta kar-gar-se
My car won't start	No arranca el coche	No a-rran-ka el ko-che
It's not running properly	No marcha bien	No mar-cha bee-en
Please change the wheel	Cambie la rueda, por favor	Kam-bee-e la rwe-da por fa-bor
This tyre is flat/punctured	Este neumático está desinflado/pinchado	Es-te ne-oo-ma-tee-ko es-ta de-seen-fla-do/peen-cha-do
The exhaust is broken	El tubo de escape está roto	El too-bo de es-ka-pe es-ta ro-to
The windscreen wipers do not work	El limpiaparabrisas no funciona	El leem-pee-a-pa-ra-bree-sas no foon-thyo-na
The valve is leaking	La válvula pierde	La bai-boo-la pee-er-de
The radiator is leaking	Gotea el radiador	Go-te-a el ra-dee-a-dor
The engine is overheating	El motor se calienta	El mo-tor se ka-lee-en-ta
The engine is firing badly	El motor funciona mal	El mo-tor foon-thyo-na mal
It's smoking	Está echando humo	Es-ta e-chan-do oo-mo

Can you change this faulty plug?	¿Puede cambiarme esta bujía estropeada?	Pwe-de kam-bee-ar-me es-ta boo-**hee**-a es-tro-pe-a-da
There's a petrol/oil leak	Pierde gasolina/ aceite	Pee-er-de gas-o-lee-na/ a-thay-te
There's a smell of petrol/rubber	Hay olor a gasolina/ goma	Eye o-lor a gas-o-lee-na/ go-ma
There's a rattle	Hace ruido	A-the roo-ee-do
Something is wrong with	Hay algo que no va bien en	Eye al-go ke no ba bee-en en
my car	mi coche	mee ko-che
the engine	el motor	el mo-tor
the lights	las luces	las loo-thes
the clutch	el embrague	el em-bra-ge
the gearbox	la caja de cambios	la ka-ha de kam-bee-os
the brakes	los frenos	los fre-nos
the steering	la dirección	la dee-rek-**thyon**
I've got electrical/ mechanical trouble	Se me ha estropeado el coche: debe ser algo eléctrico/ mecánico	Se me a es-tro-pe-a-do el ko-che de-be ser al-go el-ek-tree-ko/me-ka-nee-ko
The carburettor needs adjusting	El carburador precisa un reglaje	El kar-boo-ra-dor pre-thee-sa oon-re-gla-he
Can you repair it?	¿Pueden arreglarlo?	Pwe-den ar-re-glar-lo
How long will it take to repair?	¿Cuánto tiempo necesita para arreglarlo?	Kwan-to tee-em-po ne-the-see-ta pa-ra ar-re-glar-lo
What will it cost?	¿Cuánto costará?	Kwan-to kos-ta-**ra**
When will the car be ready?	¿Cuándo estará el coche arreglado?	Kwan-do es-ta-**ra** el ko-che ar-re-gla-do

I need it	Lo necesito-lo	Lo ne-the-see-to-lo
as soon as possible	antes posible	an-tes po-see-ble
in three hours	dentro de tres horas	den-tro de tres o-ras
in the morning	mañana por la mañana	ma-nya-na por la ma-nya-na
It will take two days	*Tardaremos dos días en arreglarlo	Tar-dar-emos dos dee-as en ar-re-glar-lo
We can repair it temporarily	*Se puede arreglar provisionalmente	Se pwe-de ar-re-glar pro-bee-syo-nal-men-te
We haven't the right spares	*No tenemos los recambios necesarios	No ten-e-mos los re-cam-byos ne-the-sa-ree-os
We have to send for the spares	*Tenemos que pedir los recambios	Ten-e-mos ke pe-deer los re-cam-byos
You will need a few ...	*Necesita un (una) ... nuevo (nueva)	Ne-thee-see-ta oon/a ... nwe-bo/a
Could I have an itemized bill, please?	¿Puede darme una factura detallada, por favor?	Pwe-de dar-me oon-a fak-too-ra de-ta-llya-da por fa-bor

PARTS OF A CAR AND OTHER USEFUL WORDS

accelerate	acelerar	a-the-le-rar
accelerator	el acelerador	a-the-le-ra-dor
airpump	la bomba de aire	bom-ba de a-ee-re
anti-freeze	el anticongelante	anti-con-he-lan-te

automatic transmission	**la transmisión automática**	trans-mee-**syon** ow-to-ma-tee-ka
axle	**el eje**	e-he
battery	**la batería**	ba-tai-**ree**-a
bonnet	**el capó**	ka-**po**
boot/trunk	**el maletero**	ma-le-ter-o
brake	**el freno**	fre-no
brake lights	**las luces del freno**	loo-thes del fre-no
brake lining	**los cojinetes del freno**	ko-hee-ne-tes del fre-no
brake pad	**la guarnición del freno**	gwar-nee-**thyon** del fre-no
breakdown	**la avería**	a-ber-**ee**-a
bulb	**la luz/bombilla**	looth/bom-bee-llya
bumper	**los parachoques**	pa-ra-cho-kes
carburettor	**el carburador**	kar-boo-ra-dor
choke	**el aire**	a-ee-re
clutch	**el embrague**	em-bra-ge
cooling system	**el sistema de refrigeración**	sees-te-ma de re-free-he-ra-**thyon**
crank-shaft	**el cigüeñal**	thee-gwe-nyal
cylinder	**el cilindro**	thee-leen-dro
differential gear	**el diferencial**	dee-fer-en-thee-al
dip stick	**el indicador de nivel de aceite**	een-dee-ka-dor de nee-bel de a-thay-te
distilled water	**el agua destilada**	a-gwa des-tee-la-da
distributor	**el distribuidor**	dee-stree-boo-ee-dor

door	**la puerta**	pwair-ta
doorhandle	**la manilla**	ma-nee-llya
drive (to)	**conducir**	kon-doo-theer
drive shaft	**el árbol de transmisión**	ar-bol de trans-mee-syon
driver	**el conductor**	kon-dook-tor
dynamo	**la dinamo**	dee-na-mo
engine	**el motor**	mo-tor
exhaust	**el (tubo de) escape**	es-ka-pe
fan	**el ventilador**	ben-tee-la-dor
fanbelt	**la correa del ventilador**	kor-re-a del ben-tee-la-dor
(oil) filter	**el filtro (de aceite)**	feel-tro
foglamp	**el antiniebla**	anti-nee-eb-la
fusebox	**la caja de fusibles**	ka-ha de foo-see-bles
gasket	**la empaquetadura**	em-pa-ke-ta-doo-ra
gearbox	**la caja de cambios/de velocidades**	ka-ha de kam-bee-os/de be-lo-thee-da-des
gear-lever	**la palanca de cambios**	pa-lan-ka de kam-bee-os
gears	**los cambios (de velocidad)**	kam-bee-os
grease (to)	**engrasar**	en-gra-sar
handbrake	**el freno de mano**	fre-no de ma-no
headlights	**las luces delanteras**	loo-thes de-lan-tair-as
heater	**la calefacción**	ka-le-fak-thy-on
horn	**la bocina/el claxon**	bo-thee-na/klak-son

hose	**el manguito**	man-gee-to
ignition key	**la llave del contacto**	llya-be del kon-tak-to
indicator	**el indicador**	een-dee-ka-dor
jack	**el gato**	ga-to
key	**la llave**	llya-be
mirror	**el espejo**	es-pe-ho
number plate	**la (placa de) matrícula**	ma-**tree**-koo-la
nut	**la tuerca**	twer-ka
oil	**el aceite**	a-thay-te
parking lights	**las luces de aparcar**	loo-thes de a-par-kar
petrol	**la gasolina**	ga-so-lee-na
petrol can	**la lata de gasolina**	la-ta de ga-so-lee-na
piston	**el émbolo**	**em**-bo-lo
plug	**la bujía**	boo-**hee**-a
points	**las conexiones**	ko-ne-see-o-nes
(oil/water) pump	**la bomba (de aceite/ agua)**	bom-ba
puncture	**el pinchazo**	peen-cha-tho
radiator	**el radiador**	ra-dee-a-dor
rear lights	**las luces traseras**	loo-thes tra-sair-as
reverse	**la marcha atrás**	mar-cha a-**tras**
reversing lights	**las luces de retroceso**	loo-thes de re-tro-the-so
(sliding) roof	**el techo (descapotable)**	te-cho
screwdriver	**el destornillador**	des-tor-nee-llya-dor
seat	**el asiento**	a-see-en-to

shock absorber	**el amortiguador**	a-mor-tee-gwa-dor
silencer	**el silenciador**	see-len-thee-a-dor
spanner	**la llave inglesa**	llya-be een-gle-sa
spares	**los recambios**	re-cam-byos
spare wheel	**la rueda de repuesto**	rwe-da de re-pwes-to
speedometer	**el cuentakilómetros**	kwen-ta-kee-lo-me-tros
spring	**el resorte/el muelle**	re-sor-te/mwe-llye
stall (to)	**atascarse**	a-tas-kar-se
steering	**la dirección**	dee-rek-thyon
steering wheel	**el volante**	bo-lan-te
suspension	**la suspensión**	soos-pen-syon
tank	**el depósito**	de-po-see-to
tappets	**los alza-válvulas**	al-tha-bal-boo-las
transmission	**la transmisión**	trans-mee-syon
tyre	**el neumático**	ne-oo-ma-tee-ko
valve	**la válvula**	bal-boo-la
wheel	**la rueda**	rwe-da
back wheel/front wheel	**la rueda de atrás/la rueda de adelante**	rwe-da de a-tras/rwe-da de a-de-lan-te
window	**la ventanilla**	ben-tan-ee-llya
windscreen	**el parabrisas**	pa-ra-bree-sas
windscreen washers	**los lavaparabrisas**	la-ba-pa-ra-bree-sas
windscreen wipers	**el limpiaparabrisas**	leem-pee-a-pa-ra-bree-sas

CYCLING

Where can I hire a bicycle?	¿Dónde puedo alquilar bicicletas?	Don-de pwe-do al-kee-lar bee-thee-klay-tas
Do you have a bicycle with gears?	¿Tiene bicicletas con cambio de velocidad?	Tee-e-ne bee-thee-klay-tas kon kam-byo de be-lod-thee-dad
The saddle is too high/too low	El sillín está muy alto/bajo	El see-llyeen es-ta mwee al-to/ba-ho
Where is the cycle shop?	¿Dónde hay una tienda de bicicletas?	Don-de eye oon-a tee-en-da de bee-thee-klay-tas
Do you repair bicycles?	¿Reparan bicicletas aquí?	Re-pa-ran bee-thee-klay-tas a-kee
The brake isn't working	El freno no funciona	El fre-no no foon-thyo-na
Could you tighten/loosen the brake cable?	¿Puede tensar/aflojar el cable del freno?	Pwe-de ten-sar/a-flo-har el ka-ble del fre-no
A spoke is broken	Un radio está roto	Oon ra-dee-o es-ta ro-to

The tyre is punctured	La rueda está pinchada	La rwe-da es-ta peen-cha-da
The gears need adjusting	Los cambios necesitan ajuste	Los kam-byos ne-the-see-tan a-hoos-te
Could you straighten the wheel?	¿Puede enderezarme el neumático?	Pwe-de en-dair-re-thar-me el ne-oo-ma-tee-ko
The handlebars are loose	El manillar está suelto	El ma-nee-llyar es-ta swel-to
Could you please lend me a spanner?	¿Me puede prestar una llave inglesa?	Me pwe-de pres-tar oon-a llya-be een-gle-sa
Could you please lend me a tyre lever?	¿Me puede prestar una palanca de neumático?	Me pwe-de pres-tar oon-a pa-lan-ka de ne-oo-ma-tee-ko

PARTS OF A BICYCLE

axle	el eje	e-he
bell	el timbre	teem-bre
brake (front/rear)	el freno (delantero/trasero)	fre-no (de-lan-te-ro/tra-se-ro)
brake cable	el cable de freno	ka-ble de fre-no
brake lever	la palanca de freno	pa-lan-ka de fre-no
bulb	la bombilla	bom-bee-llya
chain	la cadena	ka-de-na
dynamo	el dinamo	**dee**-na-mo
frame	el cuadro	kwa-dro
gear lever	el cambio de marcha	kam-byo de mar-cha
gears	los cambios	kam-byos

handlebars	**el manillar**	ma-nee-llyar
inner tube	**la llanta**	llyan-ta
light (front)	**la luz delantera**	looth de-lan-te-ra
light (rear)	**la luz trasera**	looth tra-se-ra
mudguard	**el guardabarros**	gwar-da-ba-rros
panniers	**el serón**	se-ron
pedal	**el pedal**	pe-dal
pump	**el bombín**	bom-**been**
reflector	**el reflector**	re-flek-tor
rim	**la llanta**	llyan-ta
saddle	**el sillín**	see-**llyeen**
saddlebag	**la alforja**	al-for-ha
spoke	**el radio**	**ra**-dee-o
tyre	**el neumático**	ne-oo-**ma**-tee-ko
valve	**la válvula**	**bal**-boo-la
wheel	**la rueda**	rwe-da

HOTELS & GUEST HOUSES[1]

BOOKING A ROOM

Rooms to let/vacancies	*Hay habitaciones/se alquilan habitaciones/ camas	Eye a-bee-ta-thyo-nes/se al-kee-lan a-bee-ta-thyo-nes/ka-mas
No vacancies	*(Hotel) completo	O-tel com-ple-to
Where is there a cheap hotel?	¿Dónde hay un hotel barato?	Don-de eye oon o-tel ba-ra-to
Have you a room for the night?	¿Tienen habitación para esta noche?	Tee-e-nen a-bee-ta-thyon pa-ra es-ta no-che

1. See also LAUNDRY AND DRY CLEANING (p. 131) and GOING TO A RESTAURANT (p. 83). In addition to privately owned hotels and pensions Spain also has state-run accommodation called **paradores, refugios** and **albergues de carretera**. You are not allowed to stay in an **albergue** for more than 48 hours.

How long will you be staying?	*¿Cuánto tiempo van a estar?	Kwan-to tee-em-po ban a es-tar
Is it for one night only?	*¿Sólo una noche?	So-lo oon-a no-che
Do you know another good hotel?	¿Puede recomendarme otro hotel bueno?	Pwe-de re-kom-en-dar-me ot-ro o-tel bwe-no
I've reserved a room; my name is …	Tengo habitación reservada; mi nombre es …	Ten-go a-bee-ta-thyon re-sair-ba-da mee nom-bre es
I want a single room with a shower/ private toilet	Quiero habitación individual con ducha/servicio privado	Kee-e-ro a-bee-ta-thyon een-dee-bee-doo-al kon doo-cha/sair-bee-thyo pree-ba-do
We want a room with a double bed and a bathroom	Queremos habitación con cama de matrimonio y baño	Ke-rai-mos a-bee-ta-thyon kon ka-ma de mat-ree-mon-ee-o ee ba-nyo
Have you a room with twin beds?	¿Tiene habitación de dos camas?	Tee-en-e a-bee-ta-thyon de dos ka-mas
I want a room with a washbasin	Quiero habitación con lavabo	Kee-e-ro a-bee-ta-thyon kon la-ba-bo
Is there hot and cold water?	¿Hay agua caliente y fría?	Eye a-gwa kal-ee-en-te ee free-a
I want a room for two or three days	Quiero habitación para dos o tres días	Kee-e-ro a-bee-ta-thyon pa-ra dos o tres dee-as
for a week until Friday	para una semana hasta el viernes	pa-ra oon-a se-ma-na as-ta el byair-nes
What floor is the room on?	¿En qué piso está la habitación?	En ke pee-so es-ta la a-bee-ta-thyon
Is there a lift/elevator?	¿Hay ascensor?	Eye as-then-sor

Are there facilities for the disabled?	¿Hay facilidades para los inválidos?	Eye fa-thee-lee-da-des pa-ra los een-ba-lee-dos
Have you a room on the first floor?	¿Tiene habitación en el primer piso?	Tee-en-e a-bee-ta-thyon en el pree-mair pee-so
May I see the room?	¿Puedo ver la habitación?	Pwe-do ber la a-bee-ta-thyon
I'll take this room	Tomo esta habitación	To-mo es-ta a-bee-ta-thyon
I don't like this room	No me gusta esta habitación	No me goo-sta es-ta a-bee-ta-thyon
Have you another one?	¿Tiene otra?	Tee-en-e ot-ra
I want a quiet room/a bigger room	Quiero una habitación tranquila/una habitación más grande	Kee-er-o oon-a a-bee-ta-thyon tran-kee-la/oon-a a-bee-ta-thyon mas gran-de
There's too much noise in this room	Hay mucho ruido en esta habitación	Eye moo-cho roo-ee-do en es-ta a-bee-ta-thyon
I'd like a room with a balcony	Me gustaría una habitación con balcón	Me goos-ta-ree-a oon-a a-bee-ta-thyon kon bal-kon
Have you a room looking on to the street/the sea?	¿Tiene habitación que dé a la calle/al mar?	Tee-en-e a-bee-ta-thyon ke de a la ka-llye/al mar
Is there a telephone? a radio? a television? piped music?	¿Hay teléfono? radio? televisión? hilo musical?	Eye te-le-fo-no ra-dee-o te-le-bee-syon ee-lo moo-see-kal

We've only a twin-bedded room	*Sólo tenemos habitación doble	So-lo te-ne-mos a-bee-ta-**thyon** do-ble
This is the only room vacant	*Esta es la única habitación que tenemos	Es-ta es la oo-nee-ka a-bee-ta-**thyon** ke te-ne-mos
We shall have another room tomorrow	*Tendremos otra habitación mañana	Ten-dre-mos ot-ra a-bee-ta-**thyon** ma-nya-na
The room is only available tonight	*La habitación sólo está disponible esta noche	La a-bee-ta-**thyon** so-lo es-ta dees-po-nee-ble es-ta no-che
How much is the room per day?	¿Cuánto cuesta la habitación por día?	Kwan-to kwes-ta la a-bee-ta-**thyon** por dee-a
Have you nothing cheaper?	¿No tienen habitaciones más baratas?	No tee-en-en a-bee-ta-thyo-nes mas ba-ra-tas
What do we pay for the child/children?	¿Cuánto se paga por el niño/los niños?	Kwan-to se pa-ga por el nee-nyo/los nee-nyos
Could you put a cot/an extra bed in the room?	¿Pueden poner una camita/una cama extra en la habitación?	Pwe-den po-nair oon-a ka-mee-ta/oon-a ka-ma es-tra en la a-bee-ta-thyon
Is the service (and tax) included?	¿Está todo incluido?	Es-ta to-do een-kloo-ee-do
Are meals included?	¿Están las comidas incluidas?	Es-tan las ko-mee-das een-kloo-ee-das
How much is the room without meals?	¿Cuánto es sólo la habitación?	Kwan-to es so-lo la a-bee-ta-**thyon**

How much is full board/half board?	¿Cuánto es la pensión completa/media pensión?	Kwan-to es la pen-see-on completa/ma-dee-a pen-see-on
Do you do bed and breakfast?	¿Se puede tener habitación y desayuno?	Se pwe-de te-ner a-bee-ta-thyon ee de-sa-yoo-no
What is the weekly rate?	¿Cuánto cuesta por semana?	Kwan-to kwes-ta por-se-ma-na
It's too expensive	Demasiado caro	De-ma-see-a-do ka-ro
Please fill in the registration form	*¿Pueden llenar la hoja de registro, por favor?	Pwe-den llye-nar la o-ha de re-hees-tro por fa-bor
Could I have your passport, please?	*El pasaporte, por favor	El pas-a-por-te por fa-bor

IN YOUR ROOM

chambermaid	la camarera	ka-ma-rai-ra
room service	servicio de piso	sair-bee-thyo de pee-so
I'd like breakfast in my room	Quiero el desayuno en mi habitación	Kee-ero el des-a-yoo-no en mee a-bee-ta-thyon
I'd like some ice cubes	Quiero más cubitos de hielo	Kee-e-ro mas koo-bee-tos de ee-e-lo
There's no ashtray in my room	No hay cenicero en mi habitación	No eye then-ee-thair-o en mee a-bee-ta-thyon
Can I have more hangers, please?	Quisiera más perchas, por favor	Kee-see-e-ra mas per-chas por fa-bor

Is there a point for an electric razor?	¿Hay enchufe para máquina de afeitar?	Eye en-choo-fe pa-ra ma-kee-na de a-fay-tar
What's the voltage?[1]	¿Qué voltaje hay aquí?	Ke bol-ta-he eye a-kee
Where is the bathroom?	¿Dónde está el baño?	Don-de es-ta el ba-nyo
Where is the lavatory?	¿Dónde están los servicios?	Don-de es-tan los sair-bee-thyos
Is there a shower?	¿Tienen ducha?	Tee-e-nen doo-cha
There are no towels in my room	No hay toallas en mi habitación	No eye to-a-llyas en mee a-bee-ta-thyon
There's no soap	No hay jabón	No eye ha-bon
There's no (hot) water	No hay agua (caliente)	No eye a-gwa (ka-lee-en-te)
There's no plug in my washbasin	El lavabo no tiene tapón	El la-ba-bo no tee-en-e ta-pon
The washbasin is blocked	El lavabo no corre	El la-ba-bo no kor-re
There's no toilet paper in the lavatory	No hay papel higiénico en el cuarto de baño	No eye pa-pel ee-hee-e-nee-ko en el kwar-to de ba-nyo
The lavatory won't flush	La cadena del cuarto de baño no funciona	La ka-de-na del kwar-to de ba-nyo no foon-thyo-na
The bidet leaks	El bidé gotea	El bee-de go-te-a
The light doesn't work	La luz no funciona	La looth no foon-thyo-na
The lamp is broken	La lámpara está rota	La lam-pa-ra es-ta ro-ta

1. The most usual type of current in Spain is 127 volts and 50 cycles.

The blind is stuck	**La persiana está atascada**	La pair-see-a-na es-ta a-tas-ka-da
The curtains won't close	**Las cortinas no cierran bien**	Las kor-tee-nas no thee-er-ran bee-en
May I have another blanket/another pillow, please?	**Quisiera otra manta/otra almohada, por favor**	Kee-see-air-ra o-tra man-ta/o-tra al-mo-a-da por fa-bor
The sheets on my bed haven't been changed	**No han cambiado las sábanas de mi cama**	No an kam-bee-a-do las sa-ba-nas de mee ka-ma
I can't open my window; please open it	**No puedo abrir la ventana; haga el favor de abrirla**	No pwe-do ab-reer la ben-tan-a a-ga el fa-bor de ab-reer-la
It's too hot/cold	**Hace demasiado calor/frío**	A-the de-ma-see-a-do ka-lor/**free**-o
Can the heating be turned up/down?	**¿Pueden subir/bajar un poco más la calefacción?**	Pwe-den soo-beer/ba-har oon po-ko mas la ka-le-fak-**thyon**
Can the heating be turned on/off?	**¿Pueden abrir/cerrar la calefacción?**	Pwe-den a-breer/the-rar la ka-le-fak-**thyon**
Is the room air-conditioned?	**¿Tiene la habitación aire acondicionado?**	Tee-e-ne la a-bee-ta-thyon a-ee-re a-kon-dee-thyo-na-do
The air conditioning doesn't work	**El aire acondicionado no funciona**	El a-ee-re a-kon-dee-thyo-na-do no foon-thyo-na
Come in	**Adelante/pase**	Ade-lan-te/pa-se
Put it on the table, please	**Póngalo en la mesa**	pon-ga-lo en la me-sa

How long will the laundry take?	¿Cuánto tarda la lavandería?	Kwan-to tar-da la la-ban-dair-ee-a
Have you a needle and thread?	¿Tiene aguja e hilo?	Tee-e-ne a-goo-ha e ee-lo
I want these shoes cleaned	¿Pueden limpiarme los zapatos?	Pwed-en leem-pyar-me los tha-pa-tos
Could you get this dress/suit cleaned up a bit?	¿Pueden limpiarme un poco este vestido/traje?	Pwe-den leem-pyar-me oon po-ko es-te bes-tee-do/tra-he
I want this suit pressed	¿Pueden plancharme este traje?	Pwe-den plan-char-me es-te tra-he
When will it be ready?	¿Cuándo estará?	Kwan-do es-ta-ra
It will be ready tomorrow	*Estará listo mañana	Es-ta-ra lee-sto ma-nya-na

OTHER SERVICES

porter	el portero	por-tair-o
hall porter	el conserje	kon-sair-he
page	el botones/mozo	bo-to-nes/mo-tho
manager	el gerente	he-ren-te
telephonist	la telefonista	te-le-fo-nees-ta
My key, please	La llave (de mi cuarto), por favor	La llya-be (de mee kwar-to) por fa-bor
Please wake me at 8.30	Llámeme a las ocho y media	llya-me-me a las o-cho ee me-dee-a
Please post this	Por favor ponga esto en el correo	Por fa-bor pon-ga es-to en el kor-re-o

Are there any letters for me?	¿Tengo (alguna) carta?	Ten-go (al-goon-a) kar-ta
Are there any messages for me?	¿Tengo algún recado?	Ten-go al-**goon** re-kah-do
Is there a telex?	¿Hay telex?	Eye te-lex
Can I dial direct to England/America?	¿Puedo marcar directamente a Inglaterra/ América?	Pwe-do mar-kar dee-rek-ta-men-te a Een-gla-ter-ra/Amer-ee-ka
If anyone phones, tell them I'll be back at 4.30	Si alguien llama por teléfono, digan que vuelvo a las cuatro y media	See al-gee-en llya-ma por te-**le**-fo-no dee-gan ke bwel-bo a las kwat-ro ee me-dee-a
No one telephoned	*No ha telefoneado nadie	No a te-le-fo-ne-a-do na-dee-e
There's a lady/ gentleman to see you	*Hay una señora/un señor preguntando por usted	Eye oon-a sen-yo-ra/oon sen-yor pre-goon-tan-do por oos-te
Please ask her/him to come up	Que suba a mi habitación, por favor	Ke soo-ba a mee a-bee-ta-**thyon** por fa-bor
I'm coming down (at once)	Bajo (en seguida)	Ba-ho (en se-gee-da)
Have you any writing paper? envelopes? stamps?	¿Tienen papel de escribir? sobres? sellos?	Tee-en-en pa-pel de es-kree-beer so-bres se-llyos

Can I borrow a typewriter?	¿Puede prestarme una máquina de escribir?	Pwe-de pres-tar-me oon-a ma-kee-na de es-kree-beer
Please send the chambermaid	La camarera, por favor	La ka-ma-rair-a por fa-bor
I need a guide/interpreter	Necesito un guía/un intérprete	Ne-the-see-to oon gee-a/oon een-tair-pre-te
Does the hotel have a babysitting service?	¿Tiene este hotel servicio de niñeras?	Tee-e-ne es-te o-tel sair-bee-thyo de nee-nye-ras
Can I leave this in your safe?	¿Puedo dejar esto en la caja fuerte?	Pwe-do de-har es-to en la ka-ha fwair-te
Where are the toilets?	¿Dónde están los servicios?	Don-de es-tan los sair-bee-thyos
Where is the cloakroom/the dining room?	¿Dónde está el guardarropa/el comedor?	Don-de es-ta el gwar-dar-ropa/el ko-me-dor
What time is breakfast? lunch? dinner?	¿A qué hora es el desayuno? la comida? la cena?	A ke o-ra es el des-a-yoo-no la kom-ee-da la the-na
Is there a garage?	¿Hay aquí garaje?	Eye a-kee ga-ra-he
Where can I park the car?	¿Dónde puedo aparcar el coche?	Don-de pwe-do a-par-kar el ko-che
Is the hotel open all night?	¿Está el hotel abierto toda la noche?	Es-ta el o-tel a-bee-air-to to-da la no-che
What time does it close?	¿A qué hora cierra?	A ke o-ra thee-e-ra

DEPARTURE

I'm leaving tomorrow	**Me voy mañana**	Me boy ma-nya-na
Can you have my bill ready?	**¿Quiere darme la cuenta, por favor?**	Kee-e-re dar-me la kwen-ta por fa-bor
There is a mistake on the bill	**Hay un error en la factura**	Eye oon er-ror en la fak-too-ra
Do you accept credit cards?	**¿Aceptan tarjetas de crédito?**	A-thep-tan tar-he-tas de kre-dee-to
I shall be coming back on ... Can I book a room for that date?	**Volveré el ... ¿Pueden reservarme habitación para ese día?**	Bol-be-re el ... pwe-den re-sair-bar-me a-bee-ta-thyon pa-ra es-e dee-a
Could you have my luggage brought down?	**¿Pueden bajarme el equipaje?**	Pwe-den ba-har-me el e-kee-pa-he
Please store the luggage, we will be back at ...	**Por favor guárdeme el equipaje, volveremos a ...**	Por fa-bor gwar-de-me el e-kee-pa-he bol-bair-emos a
Please order a taxi for me at 11 a.m.	**Quiero un taxi para las once**	Kee-e-ro oon ta-xi pa-ra las on-the
Thank you for a pleasant stay	**Muchas gracias por todo**	Moo-chas gra-thee-as por to-do

CAMPING

Is there a camp site nearby?	¿Hay un camping cerca?	Eye oon kam-peeng thair-ka
May we camp here?	¿Podemos hacer camping aquí?	Po-de-mos a-thair kam-peeng a-kee
in your field?	en su campo?	en soo kam-po
on the beach?	en la playa?	en la pla-ya
Where should we put our tent/caravan?	¿Dónde podemos poner la tienda/el remolque?	Don-de po-de-mos po-nair la tee-en-da/el re-mol-ke
Can I park the car next to the tent?	¿Puedo aparcar el coche al lado de la tienda?	Pwe-do a-par-kar el ko-che al la-do de la tee-en-da
Can we hire a tent on the site?	¿Podemos alquilar una tienda en el camping?	Po-de-mos al-kee-lar oon-a tee-en-da en el kam-peeng

Is/are there	¿Hay	Eye
drinking water?	**agua potable?**	a-gwa po-ta-ble
electricity?	**electricidad?**	e-lek-tree-thee-dad
showers?	**duchas?**	doo-chas
toilets?	**servicios?**	sair-bee-thee-os
a shop?	**tienda?**	tee-en-da
a swimming pool?	**piscina?**	pees-thee-na
a playground?	**columpios?**	ko-loom-pee-os
a restaurant?	**restaurante?**	res-tow-ran-te
a launderette?	**lavandería?**	la-ban-dair-ree-a

What does it cost	¿Cuánto cuesta	Kwan-to kwes-ta
per night?	**por noche?**	por no-che
per week?	**por semana?**	por se-ma-na
per person?	**por persona?**	por pair-so-na

Can I buy ice?	¿Puedo comprar hielo?	Pwe-do kom-prar ee-e-lo

Where can I buy paraffin/butane gas?	¿Dónde puedo comprar parafina/gas butano?	Don-de pwe-do kom-prar pa-ra-fee-na/gas boo-ta-no

Where do I put rubbish?	¿Dónde se pone la basura?	Don-de se po-ne la ba-soo-ra

Where can I wash up/ wash clothes?	¿Dónde puedo fregar/lavar?	Don-de pwe-do fre-gar/la-bar

Is there somewhere to dry clothes/ equipment?	¿Hay tendederos?	Eye ten-de-dair-os

My camping gas has run out	**Me he quedado sin gas**	Me e ke-da-do seen gas

The toilet is blocked	**Los servicios están embozados**	Los sair-bee-thyos es-**tan** em-bo-tha-dos

The shower doesn't work/is flooded	**La ducha no funciona/está inundada**	La doo-cha no foon-thyo-na/es-**ta** ee-noon-da-da
What is the voltage?	**¿Qué voltaje hay?**	Ke bol-ta-he eye
May we light a fire?	**¿Podemos hacer fuego?**	Po-de-mos a-thair foo-e-go
Please prepare the bill, we are leaving today	**Por favor prepare la factura, nos vamos hoy**	Por fa-bor pre-pa-re la fak-too-ra nos ba-mos oy
How long do you want to stay?	***¿Cuánto tiempo van a estar?**	Kwan-to tee-em-po ban a es-tar
What is your car registration number?	***¿Cuál es su matrícula?**	Kwal es soo ma-**tree**-koo-la
I'm afraid the camp site is full	***Lo siento el camping está lleno**	Lo see-en-to el kam-peeng es-**ta** llye-no
No camping	***Camping prohibido**	Kam-peeng pro-hee-bee-do

YOUTH HOSTELLING

How long is the walk to the youth hostel?	¿Cuánto hay a pie hasta el albergue juvenil?	Kwan-to eye a pee-e as-ta el al-bair-ge hoo-be-neel
Is there a youth hostel here?	¿Hay aquí algún albergue juvenil?	Eye a-kee al-goon al-bair-ge hoo-ben-eel
Have you a room/bed for the night?	¿Tiene habitación/cama para esta noche?	Tee-e-ne a-bee-ta-**thyon**/ka-ma pa-ra es-ta no-che
How many days can we stay?	¿Cuántos días podemos estar?	Kwan-tos **dee**-as po-de-mos es-tar
Here is my membership card	Aquí está mi carnet	A-kee es-ta mee kar-net
Do you serve meals?	¿Sirven comidas?	Seer-ben ko-mee-das
Can I use the kitchen?	¿Puedo usar la cocina?	Pwe-do oo-sar la ko-thee-na

| Is there somewhere cheap to eat nearby? | ¿Hay algún sitio barato para comer? | Eye al-**goon** see-**tee**-o ba-ra-to pa-ra ko-mer |
| I want to rent a sheet for my sleeping bag | Quiero alquilar una sábana para mi saco de dormir | Kee-e-ro al-kee-lar oon-a sa-ba-na pa-ra mee sa-ko de dor-meer |

RENTING OR OWNING A PLACE

We have rented an apartment/villa	**Hemos alquilado un apartamento/una villa**	E-mos al-kee-la-do oon a-par-ta-men-to/oon-a bee-llya
Here is our reservation	**Aquí está nuestra reserva**	A-**kee** es-ta nwes-tra re-sair-ba
Please show us around	**Por favor nos lo enseña por dentro**	Por fa-bor nos lo en-se-nya por den-tro
Does the cost include	**¿Está incluido en el precio**	Es-ta een-kloo-ee-do en el pre-thyo
electricity?	**la electricidad?**	la e-lek-tree-thee-dad?
the gas cylinder?	**la bombona del gas?**	la bom-bo-na del gas
the maid?	**la asistenta?**	a-sees-ten-ta
Which days does the maid come?	**¿Qué días viene la asistenta?**	Ke **dee**-as bee-e-ne la a-sees-ten-ta
For how long?	**¿Por cuánto tiempo?**	Por kwan-to tee-em-po

Where is	¿Dónde está	Don-de es-ta
the electricity mains switch?	la llave de la luz?	la llya-be de la looth
the water mains stopcock?	la llave del agua?	la llya-be del a-gwa
the light switch?	el interruptor de la luz?	el een-tair-roop-tor de la looth
the fusebox?	la caja de los fusibles?	la ka-ha de los foo-see-bles
the powerpoint?	están los enchufes?	es-tan los en-choo-fes
How does the heating/hot water work?	¿Cómo funciona la calefacción/el agua caliente?	Ko-mo foon-thyo-na la ka-le-fak-thyon/el a-gwa ka-lee-en-te
Is there a spare gas cylinder?	¡Hay una bombona de gas de repuesto?	Eye oon-a bom-bo-na de gas de re-pwes-to
Do gas cylinders get delivered?	¿Traen la bombona de gas a casa?	Tra-en la bom-bo-na de gas a ka-sa
Please show me how this works	Por favor enséñeme cómo funciona esto	Por fa-bor en-se-nye-me ko-mo foon-thyo-na es-to
Is there a fly screen?	¡Hay mosquitera?	Eye mos-kee-tair-a
When is the rubbish collected?	¿Cuándo recogen la basura?	Kwan-do re-ko-hen la ba-soo-ra
Where can we buy logs for the fire?	¿Dónde podemos comprar troncos para la chimenea?	Don-de po-de-mos kom-prar tron-kos pa-ra la chee-me-ne-a
Is there a barbecue?	¡Hay barbacoa?	Eye bar-ba-ko-a
Please give me another set of keys	Por favor déme otro juego de llaves	Por fa-bor de-me o-tro hwe-go de llya-bes

We have replaced the broken ...	**Hemos repuesto lo roto ...**	E-mos re-**pwes**-to lo **ro**-to
Here is the bill	***Aquí está la factura**	A-**kee** es-**ta** la fak-**too**-ra
Please return my deposit against breakages	**Por favor devuélvame la señal contra daños/roturas**	Por fa-**bor** de-**bwel**-ba-me la se-**nyal kon**-tra **da**-nyos/ro-**too**-ras

PROBLEMS

The drain is blocked	**El desagüe está embozado**	El de-sa-**gwe** es-**ta** em-bo-**tha**-do
The pipe/the sink is blocked	**La cañería/la pila está embozada**	La ka-nye-**ree**-a/la **peel**-a es-**ta** em-bo-**tha**-da
The toilet doesn't flush	**La cadena del servicio no funciona**	La ka-**de**-na del sair-**bee**-thyo no foon-**thyo**-na
There's no water	**No hay agua**	No eye **a**-gwa
We can't turn the water off/shower on	**No podemos cerrar el agua/abrir la ducha**	No po-**de**-mos the-**rrar** el **a**-gwa/a-**breer** la **doo**-cha
There is a leak/a broken window	**Hay goteras/una ventana rota**	Eye go-**te**-ras/**oon**-a ben-**ta**-na **ro**-ta
The shutters won't close	**Las persianas no cierran**	Las pair-**see**-a-nas no **thee**-er-ran
The window won't open	**La ventana no se puede abrir**	La ben-**ta**-na no se **pwe**-de a-**breer**
The electricity has gone off	**No hay luz**	No eye **looth**

The heating/cooker/ water heater doesn't work	**La calefacción/la cocina/el termo no funciona**	la ka-le-fak-**thyon**/la ko-**thee**-na/el ter-mo no foon-thyo-na
The lock is stuck	**La cerradura está atascada**	La ther-ra-doo-ra es-**ta** a-tas-ka-da
This is broken	**Esto está roto**	Es-to es-ta ro-to
This needs repairing	**Esto necesita arreglarse**	Es-to ne-the-see-ta ar-re-glar-se
The apartment/villa has been burgled	**Han robado en el apartamento/la villa**	An ro-ba-do en el a-par-ta-men-to/la bee-llya

PARTS OF THE HOUSE

balcony	**el balcón**	bal-**kon**
bathroom	**el cuarto de baño**	kwar-to de ba-nyo
bedroom	**el dormitorio**	dor-mee-to-ree-o
ceiling	**el techo**	te-cho
chimney	**la chimenea**	chee-me-ne-a
corridor	**el pasillo/el corredor**	pa-see-llyo/kor-re-dor
door	**la puerta**	pwer-ta
fence	**la valla**	ba-llya
fireplace	**la chimenea**	chee-me-ne-a
floor	**el suelo**	swe-lo
garage	**el garaje**	ga-ra-he
gate	**la puerta de jardín**	pwer-ta de har-**deen**
hall	**el vestíbulo**	bes-tee-boo-lo

kitchen	**la cocina**	ko-thee-na
living room	**el salón**	sa-lon
patio	**el patio**	pa-tyo
roof	**el techo**	te-cho
shutters	**las persianas**	pair-see-a-nas
stairs	**las escaleras**	es-ka-lair-as
terrace	**la terraza**	ter-ra-tha
wall	**la pared**	pa-red
window	**la ventana**	ben-ta-na

FURNITURE AND FITTINGS

armchair	**el sillón**	see-llyon
barbecue	**la barbacoa**	bar-ba-ko-a
bath	**la bañera**	ba-nye-ra
bed	**la cama**	ka-ma
blanket	**la manta**	man-ta
bolt (*for door*)	**el cerrojo**	ther-ro-ho
broom	**la escoba**	es-ko-ba
brush	**el cepillo**	the-pee-llyo
bucket	**el pozal**	po-thal
carpet	**la alfombra**	al-fom-bra
cassette player	**el caset**	ka-set
central heating	**la calefacción central**	ka-le-fak-**thyon** then-tral
chair	**la silla**	see-llya

charcoal	**el carbón**	kar-**bon**
clock	**el reloj**	re-**loh**
cooker	**la cocina de gas**	ko-**thee**-na de gas
cupboard	**el armario**	ar-**ma**-ree-o
cushions	**los cojines**	ko-**hee**-nes
curtains	**las cortinas**	kor-**tee**-nas
deckchair	**la tumbona/la hamaca**	toom-**bo**-na/a-**ma**-ka
door	**la puerta**	**pwer**-ta
doorbell	**el timbre de la puerta**	**teem**-bre de la **pwer**-ta
doorknob	**el pomo de la puerta**	**po**-mo de la **pwer**-ta
dustbin	**el basurero**	ba-soo-**re**-ro
dustpan	**el recogedor**	re-ko-he-**dor**
hinge	**la bisagra**	bee-**sa**-gra
immersion heater	**el calentador de agua**	ka-len-ta-**dor** de **a**-gwa
iron	**la plancha**	**plan**-cha
lamp	**la lámpara**	**lam**-pa-ra
lampshade	**la pantalla**	pan-**ta**-llya
light bulb	**la bombilla**	bom-**bee**-llya
lock	**el cerrojo**	ther-**ro**-ho
mattress	**el colchón**	kol-**chon**
mirror	**el espejo**	es-**pe**-ho
mop	**la fregona**	fre-**go**-na
padlock	**el candado**	kan-**da**-do
pillow	**el almohadón**	al-mo-ha-**don**

pipe	la cañería	ka-nye-ree-a
plug (electric)	el enchufe	en-choo-fe
plug (bath)	el tapón	ta-pon
radio	la radio	ra-dee-o
refrigerator	el refrigerador/la nevera	re-free-he-ra-dor/ne-bair-a
sheet	la sábana	sa-ba-na
shelf	la estantería	es-tan-tair-ee-a
shower	la ducha	doo-cha
sink	la pila	pee-la
sofa	el sofá	so-fa
stool	el taburete	ta-boo-re-te
sun-lounger	la tumbona	toom-bo-na
table	la mesa	me-sa
tap	el grifo	gree-fo
tiles	las baldosas	bal-do-sas
toilet	el servicio/el water	sair-bee-thyo/ba-tair
towel	la toalla	to-a-llya
vacuum cleaner	la aspiradora	as-pee-ra-do-ra
washbasin	la pila del baño	pee-la del ba-nyo
washing machine	la lavadora	la-ba-do-ra
window catch	el asidor de ventana	a-see-dor de ben-ta-na
window sill	la repisa de la ventana	re-pee-sa de la ben-ta-na

KITCHEN EQUIPMENT

bleach	**la lejía**	le-hee-a
bottle opener	**el abrebotellas**	a-bre-bo-te-llyas
bowl	**el tazón**	ta-thon
can opener	**el abrelatas**	a-bre-la-tas
candle	**la vela**	be-la
clothes line	**el tendedero**	ten-de-dero
clothes peg	**la pinza de la ropa**	peen-tha de la ro-pa
chopping board	**el tajo**	ta-ho
coffee pot	**la cafetera**	ka-fe-te-ra
colander	**el escurridor**	es-koo-ree-dor
coolbox	**la nevera hielo**	ne-be-ra ee-e-lo
corkscrew	**el sacacorchos**	sa-ka-kor-chos
cup	**la taza**	ta-tha
detergent	**el detergente**	de-tair-hen-te
fork	**el tenedor**	te-ne-dor
frying pan	**la sartén**	sar-ten
glass	**el vaso**	ba-so
ice tray	**la bandeja para el hielo**	ban-de-ha pa-ra el ee-e-lo
kettle	**la tetera para calentar agua**	te-te-ra pa-ra ka-len-tar a-gwa
knife	**el cuchillo**	koo-chee-llyo
matches	**las cerillas**	the-ree-llyas
pan	**el cazo**	ka-tho

plate	**el plato**	pla-to
scissors	**las tijeras**	tee-her-as
sieve	**la coladera**	ko-la-de-ra
spoon	**la cuchara**	koo-cha-ra
teatowel	**el paño de cocina**	pan-yo de ko-thee-na
torch	**la linterna**	leen-ter-na
washing powder	**el detergente**	de-tair-hen-te
washing-up liquid	**el detergente de lavavajillas**	de-tair-hen-te de la-ba-ba-hee-llyas

ODD JOBS[1]

bracket	**la escuadra/el soporte**	es-koo-a-dra/so-por-te
cement	**el cemento**	the-men-to
hammer	**el martillo**	mar-tee-llyo
iron	**la plancha**	plan-cha
laquer	**el laqueador**	la-ke-a-dor
metal	**el metal**	me-tal
nails	**los clavos/las puntas**	kla-bos/poon-tas
paint	**la pintura**	peen-too-ra
paint brush	**la brocha**	bro-cha
plaster	**la escayola**	es-ka-yo-la
plastic	**el plástico**	**plas**-tee-ko
pliers	**las tenazas**	te-na-thas

1. See also SHOPPING & SERVICES, p. 110.

saw	**la sierra**	see-e-rra
screwdriver	**el destornillador**	des-tor-nee-llya-dor
screws	**los tornillos**	tor-nee-llyos
spanner	**la llave inglesa**	llya-be een-gle-sa
steel	**el acero**	a-the-ro
tile	**la baldosa**	bal-do-sa
wire	**el alambre**	a-lam-bre
wood	**la madera**	ma-de-ra

MEETING PEOPLE

May I introduce ...?	**Permítame que le presente ...**	Pair-mee-ta-me ke le pre-sen-te
Have you met ...?	**¿Conoce usted a ...?**	Ko-no-the oos-te a
Glad to meet you	**Encantado**	En-kan-ta-do
How are you/things?	**¿Cómo está(n)?**	Ko-mo es-ta/es-tan
Fine, thanks, and you?	**Muy bien, gracias y usted?**	Mwee bee-en gra-thee-as ee oos-te
What is your name?	**¿Cómo se llama?**	Ko-mo se llya-ma
My name is ...	**Soy .../Me llamo ...**	Soy .../Me llya-mo
This is ...	**Este señor/esta señora es ...**	Es-te se-nyor/es-ta se-nyo-ra es ...
Am I disturbing you?	**¿Le molesto?**	Le mo-les-to
Go away	**Márchese**	**Mar-che-se**
Leave me alone	**Déjeme en paz**	**De-he-me en path**
Sorry to have troubled you	**Siento molestar**	See-en-to mo-les-tar

MAKING FRIENDS

Do you live/are you staying here?	¿Vive/está usted aquí?	Bee-be/es-ta oos-te a-kee
Do you travel a lot?	¿Viaja usted mucho?	Bee-a-ha oos-te moo-cho
We've been here a week	Estamos aquí ya una semana	Es-ta-mos a-kee ya oon-a se-ma-na
Is this your first time here?	¿Es la primera vez que está aquí?	Es la pree-mair-a beth ke es-ta a-kee
Do you like it here?	¿Le gusta esto?	Le goo-sta es-to
Are you on your own?	¿Está solo/sola?	Es-ta so-lo/so-la
I am with my husband my wife my parents my family a friend	Estoy con mi marido mi esposa mis padres mi familia un amigo	Es-toy kon mee ma-ree-do mee es-po-sa mees pa-dres mee fa-mee-lee-a oon a-mee-go
I am travelling alone	Viajo solo/sola	Bee-a-ho so-lo/so-la
Where do you come from?	¿De dónde es usted?	De don-de es oos-te
I come from ...	Soy de ...	Soy de ...
What do you do?	¿Qué hace usted?	Ke a-the oos-te
What are you studying?	¿Qué estudia?	Ke es-too-dee-a
I'm on holiday/a business trip	Estoy de vacaciones/de negocios	Es-toy de ba-ka-thyo-nes/de ne-go-thyos
Are you married/single?	¿Está usted casado/soltero?	Es-ta oos-te ka-sa-do/sol-tair-o
Do you have children?	¿Tiene hijos?	Tee-e-ne ee-hos

Have you been to England/America?	**¿Ha estado usted en Inglaterra/ América?**	A es-ta-do oos-te en Een-gla-te-rra/A-me-ree-ka
I hope to see you again	**Espero volver a verlo**	Es-pe-ro bol-bair a bair-lo
Do you smoke?	**¿Fuma?**	Foo-ma
No, I don't, thanks	**No gracias**	No gra-thee-as
Help yourself	**Sírvase**	Seer-ba-se
Can I get you a drink?	**¿Puedo ofrecerle algo de beber?**	Pwe-do o-fre-thair-le al-go de be-ber
I'd like a … please	**Quisiera un … por favor**	Kee-see-er-a oon … por fa-bor

INVITATIONS[1]

Would you like to have lunch tomorrow?	**¿Le gustaría comer conmigo mañana?**	Le goos-tar-ee-a ko-mair kon-mee-go ma-nya-na
Can you come to dinner/for a drink?	**¿Puede venir a cenar/a tomar una copa (unos vinos)?**[2]	Pwe-de be-neer a the-nar/a to-mar oon-a ko-pa (oon-os bee-nos)
We are giving a party/ there is a party; would you like to come?	**Damos/hay una fiesta (un guateque); ¿quieres venir?**[3]	Da-mos/eye oon-a fee-es-ta (oon wa-te-ke) kee-e-res be-nir

1. Elsewhere in the book the polite form for 'you' has been used. Since this section deals with close personal relationships we have usually used the familiar form **tu**.
2. **Una copa** is quite formal; **unos vinos** is more commonly used by young people.
3. **Una fiesta** is a formal party; **un guateque** an informal party.

May I bring a (girl) friend?	¿Puedo ir con un amigo (una amiga)?	Pwe-do eer kon oon a-mee-go (oon-a a-mee-ga)
Thanks for the invitation	Gracias por la invitación	Gra-thee-as por la een-bee-ta-**thyon**
I'd love to come	Tendré mucho gusto en venir	Ten-drai moo-cho goos-to en be-neer
I'm sorry, I can't come	Lo siento, no puedo ir	Lo see-en-to, no pwe-do eer
Are you doing anything tonight/tomorrow afternoon?	¿Tienes plan esta noche/mañana por la tarde?	Tee-e-nes pl-an es-ta no-che/ma-nya-na por la tar-de
Could we have coffee/a drink somewhere?	¿Podemos tomar café/una copa (unos vinos) en algún sitio?[1]	Po-de-mos to-mar ka-fe/oon-a ko-pa (oon-os bee-nos) en al-goon see-tee-o
Shall we go to the cinema/theatre/beach?	¿Vamos al cine/al teatro/a la playa?	Ba-mos al thee-ne/al te-a-tro/a la pla-ya
Would you like to go dancing/for a drive?	¿Quieres que vayamos a bailar/a dar un paseo en coche?	Kee-e-res ke ba-ya-mos a ba-ee-lar/a dar oon pa-se-o en ko-che
Do you know a good disco/restaurant?	¿Sabes cual es una buena discoteca/un buen restaurante?	Sa-bes kwal es oon-a bwe-na dees-ko-te-ka bwen res-tow-ran-te
Where shall we meet?	¿Dónde nos encontramos?	Don-de nos en-kon-tra-mos

1. See note 2, p. 80.

What time shall I/we come?	¿A qué hora vengo/ venimos?	A ke o-ra ben-go/be-nee-mos
I could pick you up at (*place/time*)	Puedo recogerte en ... a las ...	Pwe-do re-ko-her-te en ... a las ...
Could you meet me at the hotel?	¿Puedes encontrarme en el hotel?	Pwe-des en-kon-trar-me en el o-tel
May I see you home?	¿Puedo acompañarte?	Pwe-do a-kom-pa-nyar-te
Can we give you a lift home/to your hotel?	¿Podemos llevarte en el coche a tu casa/a tu hotel?	Po-de-mos llye-bar-te en el ko-che a too ka-sa/a too o-tel
May I see you again?	¿Puedo verte otra vez?	Pwe-do bair-te ot-ra beth
Where do you live?	¿Dónde vives?	Don-de bee-bes
What is your telephone number?	¿Cuál es tu teléfono?	Kwal es too te-le-fono
Thanks for the drinks/ride	Gracias por la copa/ el paseo	Gra-thee-as por la ko-pa/el pa-seo
It was lovely	Ha sido muy agradable	A see-do mwee a-gra-da-ble
It was nice talking to you	Ha sido muy agradable charlar contigo	A see-do mwee a-gra-da-ble char-lar kon-tee-go
Hope to see you again soon	Espero verte pronto	Es-pair-o bair-te pron-to
See you soon/ tomorrow	Hasta luego/hasta mañana	As-ta lwe-go/as-ta ma-nya-na

GOING TO A RESTAURANT

Can you suggest	¿Puede recomendarnos	Pwe-de re-kom-men-dar-nos
a good restaurant?	un buen restaurante?	oon bwen res-tow-ran-te
a cheap restaurant?	un restaurante económico?	oon res-tow-ran-te eko-no-mee-ko
a vegetarian restaurant?	un restaurante vegetariano?	oon res-tow-ran-te be-he-ta-ree-ano
I'd like to book a table for four at 1 p.m.	Quisiera reservar mesa para cuatro para la una	Kee-see-era re-sair-bar me-sa pa-ra kwa-tro pa-ra la oona
I've reserved a table; my name is ...	Tengo mesa reservada a nombre de ...	Ten-go me-sa re-sair-ba-da a nom-bre de ...
Have you reserved a table?	*¿Han reservado una mesa?	An re-sair-ba-do oon-a me-sa
We did not make a reservation	No hemos reservado	No em-os re-sair-ba-do
Have you a table for three?	¿Hay una mesa para tres?	Eye oon-a me-sa pa-ra tr-es

Is there a table on the terrace? by the window? in a corner?	¿Hay mesa en la terraza? junto al ventanal? en un rincón?	Eye me-sa en la ter-ra-tha hoon-to al ben-ta-nal en oon reen-kon
Is there a non-smoking area?	¿Hay zona de no fumadores?	Eye tho-na de no foo-ma-do-res
We are in a (great) hurry	Tenemos (mucha) prisa	Te-ne-mos (moo-cha) pree-sa
This way, please	*Por aquí, por favor	Por a-kee, por fa-bor
We shall have a table free in half an hour	*Habrá mesa dentro de media hora	A-bra me-sa den-tro de me-dee-a o-ra
You will have to wait about ... minutes	*Tendrán que esperar unos ... minutos	Ten-dran ke es-pe-rar oon-os ... mee-noo-tos
We don't serve lunch until 1 p.m.[1]	*La comida no se sirve hasta la una	La ko-mee-da no se seer-be as-ta la oon-a
We don't serve dinner until 9 p.m.	*No se sirven cenas hasta las nueve	No se seer-ben then-as as-ta las nwe-be
Last orders at 4 o'clock	*El último servicio es a las cuatro	El ool-tee-mo sair-bee-thee-o es a las kwa-tro
Do you serve snacks?	¿Sirven platos combinados/ bocadillos/ pinchos?[2]	Seer-ben pla-tos kom-bee-na-dos/bo-ka-dee-llyos/peen-chos

1. In Spain lunch is usually served from 1 p.m. to 4 p.m.; dinner from 8 p.m. to 11 p.m. Bars and cafés usually stay open until about 2 a.m.
2. A **plato combinado** is a main dish served in bars and cafés. It consists of various types of meat, vegetables, fish, eggs, etc., in different combinations. **Bocadillos** are more substantial than English sandwiches, consisting of half a Vienna loaf filled with meat, omelette, etc. **Pinchos** are quite substantial side dishes or hors d'œuvres which can make a meal in themselves.

Sorry, the kitchen is closed	*Lo siento la cocina está cerrada	Lo see-en-to la ko-thee-na es-ta ther-ra-da
Where is the lavatory?	¿Dónde están los servicios?	Don-de es-tan los sair-bee-thyos
It is downstairs/upstairs	*Están abajo/arriba	Es-tan a-ba-ho/ar-ree-ba

ORDERING

waiter/waitress	camarero/camarera	ka-ma-rair-ro/ka-ma-rair-ra
Service (not) included	Servicio (no) incluido	Sair-bee-thee-o (no) een-kloo-ee-do
May I see the menu, please?	El menú/la carta, por favor	El me-noo/la kar-ta, por fa-bor
May I see the wine list, please?	La lista de vinos, por favor	La lee-sta de bee-nos, por fa-bor
Is there a set menu?[1]	Tienen menú del día/menú turístico?	Tee-e-nen me-noo del dee-a/me-noo too-ree-stee-ko
I want something light	Quiero algo ligero	Kee-er-o al-go lee-he-ro
Do you have children's helpings?	¿Hay media ración/reducción para niños?	Eye me-dee-a ra-thyon/re-dook-thyon pa-ra nee-nyos
What is your dish of the day?	¿Cuál es el plato del día?	Kwal es el pla-to del dee-a

1. The **cubierto** is the all-in price of a meal, including wine, bread and sweet. Service is always included, though it is customary to leave a small tip. There is no cover charge in Spanish restaurants.

What do you recommend?	¿Qué recomienda?	Ke re-ko-mee-en-da
Can you tell me what this is?	¿Por favor, qué es ésto?	Por fa-bor ke es es-to
What is the speciality of the restaurant?	¿Cuál es la especialidad de la casa?	Kwal es la es-pe-thee-a-lee-dad de la ka-sa
What is the speciality of the region?	¿Cuál es el plato típico de la región?	Kwal es el pla-to tee-pee-ko de la reg-ee-on
Do you have any local dishes/vegetarian dishes?	¿Tiene algún plato típico/vegetariano?	Tee-e-ne al-**goon** pla-to tee-pee-ko be-he-ta-ree-a-no
Would you like to try ...?	*¿Quiere probar ...?	Kee-ere pro-bar
There's no more ...	*No quedan ...	No ke-dan
I'd like ...	Quiero ...	Kee-ero
Is it hot or cold?	¿Es este plato caliente o frío?	Es es-te pla-to ka-lee-en-te o **free**-o
Without oil/sauce, please	Sin aceite/sin salsa, por favor	Seen a-**thay**-te/seen sal-sa por fa-bor
Some more bread, please	Más pan, por favor	Mas pan, por fa-bor
Could we have some salt, please?	Queremos sal, por favor	Ke-rai-mos sal por fa-bor

COMPLAINTS

| Where are our drinks? | ¿Dónde están nuestras bebidas? | Don-de es-**tan** nwes-tras be-bee-das |

Why is the food taking so long?	¿Por qué tardan tanto en servir la comida?	Por ke tar-dan tan-to en sair-beer la com-ee-da
This isn't what I ordered, I want ...	Esto no es lo que he pedido, quiero ...	Es-to no es lo ke e ped-ee-do, kee-e-ro
A little more ...	Un poco más ...	Oon po-ko mas
This is bad stale tough too cold salty undercooked overcooked	No está bueno pasado duro demasiado frío salado poco hecho demasiado hecho	No es-ta bwe-no pa-sa-do doo-ro de-ma-see-a-do free-o sa-la-do po-ko e-cho de-ma-see-a-do e-cho
This isn't fresh	Esto no es fresco	Es-to no es fres-ko
This plate/knife/glass is not clean	Este plato/cuchillo/vaso no está limpio	Es-te pla-to/koo-chee-llyo/ba-so no es-ta leem-pee-o
This spoon is not clean	Este cuchara no está limpia	Es-te koo-cha-ra no es-ta leem-pee-a
I'd like to see the headwaiter	Quiero ver al maitre	Kee-e-ro bair al me-tre

PAYING

| The bill, please | La cuenta, por favor | La kwen-ta por fa-bor |
| Please check the bill – I don't think it's correct | Revise la cuenta, por favor, creo que no está bien | Re-bee-se la kwen-ta por fa-bor kre-o ke no es-ta bee-en |

What is this amount for?	¿De qué es esta cantidad?	De ke es es-ta kan-tee-dad
I didn't have soup	No he tomado sopa	No e tom-ado so-pa
I had chicken, not lamb	Tomé pollo y no cordero	To-me po-llyo ee no kor-dair-o
May we have separate bills?	¿Puede darme la cuenta por separado?	Pwe-de dar-me la kwen-ta por se-pa-ra-do
Is service included?	¿El servicio está incluido?	El sair-bee-thee-o es-ta een-kloo-ee-do
Can I pay with travellers' cheques/a credit card?	¿Puedo pagar con cheque de viajero/tarjeta de crédito?	Pwe-do pa-gar kon che-ke de bya-hair-o/tar-he-ta de kre-dee-to
We enjoyed it, thank you	Gracias, nos ha gustado mucho	Gra-thee-as nos a goos-ta-do moo-cho
That was a good meal, thank you	La comida estaba muy buena gracias	La ko-mee-da es-ta-ba mwee bwe-na gra-thee-as
Keep the change	Quédese el cambio	Ke-de-se el kam-bee-o

BREAKFAST AND TEA

A large white coffee	Un café con leche doble	Oon ka-fe kon le-che do-ble
A black coffee	Un café solo	Oon ka-fe so-lo
I would like decaffeinated coffee	Quiero café descafeinado	Kee-e-ro ka-fe des-ka-fay-na-do

I would like tea with (cold) milk/lemon	Un té con leche (fría)/limón	Oon te kon le-che (**free-a**)/lee-mon
I would like a herb tea	Quiero una infusión de hierbas	Kee-e-ro oon-a een-foo-syon de ee-er-bas
May we have some sugar, please?	Azúcar por favor	A-**thoo**-kar por fa-bor
Do you have artificial sweeteners?	¿Tiene sacarina?	Tee-e-ne sa-ka-ree-na
hot/cold milk	leche caliente/fría	le-che kal-yen-te/**free-a**
bread and butter	pan y mantequilla	pan ee man-te-kee-llya
toast	tostadas	tos-ta-das
More butter, please	Más mantequilla, por favor	Mas man-te-kee-llya por fa-bor
Have you some jam?	¿Tienen mermelada?	Tee-e-nen mair-me-la-da
I'd like a soft-boiled/ hard boiled egg	Un huevo pasado por agua/cocido	Oon gwe-bo pa-sa-do por a-gwa/ko-thee-do
Bacon and egg, please	Beicon y huevo, por favor	Be-ee-kon ee gwe-bo por-fa-bor
What fruit juices have you?	¿Qué zumos de frutas tienen?	Ke thoo-mos de froo-tas tee-e-nen
orange/grapefruit/ tomato juice	zumo de naranja/ pomelo/tomate	thoo-mo de na-ran-ha/ po-me-lo/to-mat-e
drinking chocolate	el chocolate hecho	cho-ko-la-te e-cho
doughnut	el churro	choor-ro
honey	la miel	mee-el
cake	el pastel/la tarta	pas-tel/tar-ta
cereal	los cereales	the-rai-a-les
fresh fruit	la fruta	froo-ta

| yogurt | el yogurt | yo-goort |
| Help yourself at the buffet | *Sírvase usted mismo | Seer-ba-se oos-te mees-mo |

SNACKS AND PICNICS[1]

Can I have a ... sandwich, please?	Un sandwich ... por favor	Oon sand-weech ... por fa-bor
What are those things over there?	¿Qué es eso que hay ahí?	Ke es es-o ke eye eye-ee
What are they made of?	¿De qué está hecho?	De ke es-ta e-cho
What is in them?	¿Qué tiene dentro?	Ke tee-e-ne den-tro
I'll have one of those, please	Uno de esos, por favor	Oo-no de e-sos por fa-bor
It's to take away	Es para llevar	Es pa-ra llye-bar
biscuits	galletas	ga-llye-tas
bread	pan	pan
cheese	queso	ke-so
chips	patatas fritas	pa-ta-tas free-tas
chocolate bar	chocolatina	cho-ko-la-tee-na
cold cuts	fiambres	fee-am-bres
eggs	huevos	gwe-bos
boiled	cocidos	ko-thee-dos
fried	fritos	free-tos
scrambled	revueltos	re-bwel-tos

1. See footnote, p.84.

ham	**jamón**	ha-**mon**
ice cream	**helado**	e-la-do
light meals	**platos ligeros/ pinchos**	pla-tos lee-he-ros/peen-chos
meatballs	**albóndigas**	al-**bon**-dee-gas
omelette	**tortilla**	tor-tee-llya
pasties (filled with meat or fish)	**empanadillas**	em-pa-na-dee-llyas
pastries	**empanadas**	em-pa-na-das
roll	**panecillo**	pa-ne-thee-llyo
sandwich	**bocadillo/sandwich**	bo-ka-dee-llyo/sand-weech
toasted sandwich	**bocadillo caliente**	bo-ka-dee-llyo ka-lee-en-te

DRINKS[1]

bar	**el bar**	bar
café	**el café**	ka-fe
What will you have to drink?	*¿**Qué quieren beber?**	Ke kee-er-en be-bair
A bottle of the local wine, please	**Una botella de vino de la tierra**	Oon-a bo-te-llya de bee-no de la tee-er-ra
The wine list please	**La lista de vinos por favor**	La lee-sta de bee-nos por fa-bor

1. For the names of beverages, see p.106.

carafe/glass	la jarra (de vino)/el vaso	la har-ra (de bee-no)/el ba-so
bottle/half bottle	una botella/media botella	oon-a bo-te-llya/me-dee-a bo-te-llya
good quality wine	vino de marca	bee-no de mar-ka
vintage wine	vino de reserva	bee-no de re-sair-ba
Three glasses of beer, please	Tres cervezas, por favor	Tres thair-be-thas por fa-bor
Do you have draught beer?	¿Tienen cerveza de barril?	Tee-en-en thair-be-tha de bar-reel
Two more beers	Dos cervezas más	Dos thair-be-thas mas
large/small beer	cerveza grande/pequeña	thair-be-tha gran-de/pe-ke-nya
soft drinks	refrescos	re-fres-kos
Do you serve cocktails?	¿Tienen cocktails?	Tee-e-nen kok-te-les
I'd like a drink with ice	Quiero un refresco con hielo	Kee-e-ro oon re-fres-ko kon ee-e-lo
apple juice	el zumo de manzana	thoo-mo de man-tha-na
orange juice	el zumo de naranja	thoo-mo de na-ran-ha
fruit juice	el zumo de frutas	thoo-mo de froo-tas
milk shake	el batido de leche	ba-tee-do de le-che
iced coffee	el café helado	ka-fe e-la-do
hot chocolate	el chocolate hecho	cho-ko-la-te e-cho
iced tea	el té helado	te e-la-do
I'd like another glass of water	Otro vaso de agua, por favor	O-tro ba-so de a-gwa por fa-bor
neat/on the rocks	solo/con hielo	so-lo/kon ee-e-lo
with soda water	con soda	kon so-da

mineral water (still/fizzy)	**agua mineral (sin gas/con gas)**	a-gwa meen-e-ral (seen gas/kon gas)
ice (cubes)	**(cubos de) hielo**	(koo-bos de) ee-e-lo
Cheers!	**¡Salud!**	Sa-lood
The same again, please	**Lo mismo**	Lo mees-mo
Three black coffees and one with milk	**Tres cafés solos y uno con leche**	Tres ka-fes so-los ee oo-no kon le-che
Coffee with a dash of milk	**Un cortado**	Oon kor-ta-do
Tea with milk/lemon	**Té con leche/limón**	Te kon le-che/lee-**mon**
A cup of China tea	**Una taza de té chino**	Oo-na ta-tha de te chee-no
A cup of Indian tea	**Una taza de té indio**	Oo-na ta-tha de te een-dee-o
May we have an ashtray?	**Un cenicero, por favor**	Oon the-nee-thair-o por fa-bor
Can I have a light, please?	**Una cerilla, por favor**	Oo-na the-ree-llya por fa-bor

RESTAURANT VOCABULARY

artificial sweetener	**la sacarina**	sa-ka-ree-na
ashtray	**el cenicero**	then-ee-thair-o
beer	**la cerveza**	thair-be-tha
bill	**la cuenta**	kwen-ta
bread	**el pan**	pan
butter	**la mantequilla**	man-te-kee-llya
cigar	**el puro**	poo-roh

cigarettes	**los cigarrillos/pitillos**	thee-gar-ree-llyos/pee-tee-llyos
cloakroom	**el guardarropa**	gwar-dar-ropa
coffee	**el café**	ka-fe
course/dish	**el plato**	pla-to
cup	**la taza**	ta-tha
fork	**el tenedor**	te-ne-dor
glass	**el vaso**	ba-so
headwaiter	**el maitre**	me-tre
hungry (to be)	**tener hambre**	te-nair am-bre
jug of water	**la jarra de agua**	har-ra de a-gwa
knife	**el cuchillo**	koo-chee-llyo
lemon	**el limón**	lee-mon
matches	**las cerillas**	the-ree-llyas
mayonnaise	**la mayonesa**	ma-yo-ne-sa
menu	**el menú**	me-noo
mustard	**la mostaza**	mos-ta-tha
napkin	**la servilleta**	sair-bee-llye-ta
oil	**el aceite**	a-thay-te
pepper	**la pimienta**	pee-mee-en-ta
plate	**el plato**	pla-to
restaurant	**el restaurante**	res-tow-ran-te
salt	**la sal**	sal
sauce	**la salsa**	sal-sa
saucer	**el platito**	pla-tee-to
service	**el servicio**	sair-bee-thee-o

spoon	**la cuchara**	koo-cha-ra
sugar	**el azúcar**	a-thoo-kar
table	**la mesa**	me-sa
tablecloth	**el mantel**	man-tel
thirsty (to be)	**tener sed**	te-nair sed
tip	**la propina**	pro-pee-na
toothpick	**el palillo**	pal-ee-llyo
vegetarian	**vegetariano**	be-he-ta-ree-a-no
vinegar	**el vinagre**	bee-na-gray
waiter	**el camarero**	ka-ma-rair-o
waitress	**la camarera**	ka-ma-rair-a
water	**el agua**	ag-wa

THE MENU

ENTREMESES Y TAPAS[1]

aceitunas	olives
alcachofas	artichokes
anchoas	anchovies
anguilas	baby eels
arenques	herring
boquerones/chanquetes	fresh anchovies
caracoles	snails
chorizo	spicy sausage
salad	ensalada
ensaladilla rusa	Russian salad
entremeses variados	mixed hors d'œuvres

1. Tapas (hors d'œuvres) can be ordered in most Spanish bars to accompany drinks. Look at what is available and make your choice.

espárragos	asparagus
fiambres	cold cuts
gambas	prawns
gambas al ajillo	prawns with oil and garlic
gambas a la plancha	grilled prawns
huevos rellenos	stuffed eggs
jamón serrano	cured ham
jamón de york	boiled ham
melón	melon
ostras	oysters
percebes	goose barnacles
quisquillas	shrimps
sardinas	sardines

SOPAS

caldo/consomé	consommé
caldo de gallina	chicken consommé
cocido madrileño	meat and vegetable soup/stew
consomé al jerez	consommé with sherry
gazpacho	cold soup of tomatoes, cucumber, olive oil, garlic, etc.
sopa de ajo	garlic soup with bread, egg and meat
sopa de cebolla	onion soup
sopa de fideos	noodle soup
sopa de gallina	chicken soup

sopa de mariscos	shellfish soup
sopa de pescado	fish soup
sopa de verduras	vegetable soup

PESCADOS

almejas	clams
anguila	eel
atún/bonito	fresh tunny
bacalao	(dried) cod
bacalao a la vizcaína	cod stewed with olive oil, peppers, onion and tomatoes
bacalao al pil-pil	cod stewed in olive oil to produce a thick, rich sauce
besugo	sea bream
calamares	squid
calamares a la romana	squid fried in batter
calamares en su tinta	squid cooked in their own ink
cangrejo (de mar)	crab
cangrejo (de río)	crayfish
centolla	spider crab
chipirones	baby squid
gambas	prawns
langosta	lobster
lenguado	sole
mariscos	seafood

mejillones	mussels
merluza	hake
mero	grouper
ostras	oysters
pescado frito	mixed fried fish
pez espada	swordfish
pulpo	octopus
quisquillas	shrimps
rape	monkfish
raya	skate
rodaballo	turbot
salmón	salmon
salmonete	red mullet
sardinas a la plancha	sardines 'grilled' on the hot plate
sardinas en escabeche	pickled sardines
sepia	cuttlefish
vieiras	scallops
zarzuela	fish and sea food in a sauce of tomatoes, onions, garlic, bay leaves, olive oil and wine

CARNE

albóndigas	meatballs/rissoles in a spicy sauce
butifarra con judías	pork sausage with beans
cabrito	kid

callos	tripe
carnero	mutton
cerdo	pork
chorizo	sausage made from spiced, cured pig meat
chuleta	chop
cochinillo	sucking pig
cola de buey	oxtail
cordero asado	roast lamb
embutidos	spicy sausages (served cold)
escalope	escalope
estofado	stew
fabada	black pudding and bean stew
filete	fillet/cutlet
guisado de ternera	veal stew
hígado	liver
jamón	ham
lacón con grelos	shoulder of pork with turnip tops
lengua	tongue
lechazo	young lamb
lomo	loin of pork
mollejas	sweetbreads
morcilla	black pudding
pote gallego	hotpot
riñones (al jerez)	kidneys (with sherry)
salchichas	sausages (served hot)

sesos (huecos)	brains (fried)
solomillo de cerdo	pork fillet
ternera	veal
tostón	sucking pig
vaca	beef

AVES Y CAZA

carne de venado	venison
conejo	rabbit
faisán	pheasant
ganso	goose
liebre	hare
pato	duck
pavo	turkey
pechuga	chicken breast
perdiz	partridge
pichones	pigeons
pollo	chicken

ARROZ

arroz catalana	rice with pork, spicy sausages and fish
arroz con azafrán	saffron rice
arroz marinera	rice with seafood

paella valenciana	saffron rice with chicken and seafood
pollo con arroz	rice with chicken

LEGUMBRES Y VERDURAS

ajo	garlic
alcachofa	artichoke
alubias	beans
apio	celery
berenjena	aubergine/eggplant
cebolla	onion
champiñón	cultivated mushroom
coles de bruselas	Brussels sprouts
coliflor	cauliflower
escarola	endive
espárragos	asparagus
espinacas	spinach
garbanzos	chickpeas
guisantes	peas
habas	broad beans
judías verdes	green beans
lechuga	lettuce
lentejas	lentils
nabo	turnip
patata	potato

pepino	cucumber
perejil	parsley
pimiento	pepper
puerro	leek
rábano	radish
remolacha	beetroot
repollo	cabbage
seta	mushroom
tomate	tomato
zanahoria	carrot

HUEVOS

cocidos/duros	hard-boiled
escalfados	poached
fritos	fried
huevos a la flamenca	eggs baked with onion, tomato and ham
pasados por agua	soft-boiled
revueltos	scrambled
tortilla de champiñones	mushroom omelette
tortilla de espárragos	asparagus omelette
tortilla de habas	broad bean omelette
tortilla de patata	potato omelette
tortilla francesa	plain omelette

QUESO

burgos	soft creamy cheese from Burgos
cabrales	strong cheese made from ewe's milk
mahón	fairly bland hard cheese from Menorca
manchego	hard cheese made from ewe's milk in La Mancha
roncal	sharp tasting smoked cheese made from ewe's milk in northern Spain

POSTRES

almendrado	macaroon
buñuelos	fritters
compota	compote
flan	crème caramel
granizado	water ice
helado	ice cream
de café	coffee
de chocolate	chocolate
de fresa	strawberry
de vainilla	vanilla
mantecado	enriched ice cream
mazapán	marzipan
melocotón en almíbar	peaches in syrup
merengue	meringue

natilla	Spanish custard
pastel/tarta	cake
tarta helada	ice cream cake
turrón	kind of nougat
yemas	candied egg yolks

FRUTAS Y NUECES

albaricoque	apricot
almendra	almond
avellana	hazelnut
cereza	cherry
chirimoya	custard apple
ciruela	plum
dátiles	dates
fresa	strawberry
higo	fig
limón	lemon
manzana	apple
melocotón	peach
membrillo	quince
naranja	orange
níspero	loquat
pasas	raisins
pera	pear
piña	pineapple

plátano	banana
pomelo	grapefruit
sandía	water-melon
toronja	grapefruit
uvas	grapes

BEBIDAS

agua	water
agua mineral	mineral water
anís	anise
batido de leche	milk shake
cava	sparkling wine
cerveza	beer
negra	dark
de botella	bottled
de lata	in a can
de barril	draught
chocolate hecho	hot chocolate
coñac	brandy
gaseosa	fizzy drink/lemonade
ginebra	gin
horchata	cold drink made from chufa root (tiger nut)

infusiones	herb tea
manzanilla	camomile
menta/poleo	mint
rosas	rose hip
tila	lime
leche	milk
limonada	lemonade
naranjada	orangeade
ron	rum
sangría	red wine mixed with lemonade (or champagne), served with ice cubes and slices of lemon and orange
sidra	cider
té chino	China tea
té indio	Indian tea
vino	wine
blanco	white
dulce	sweet
espumoso	sparkling
rosado	rosé
seco	dry
tinto	red
zumos de frutas	fruit juices
zumo de manzana	apple juice
zumo de naranja	orange juice
zumo de pomelo	grapefruit juice
zumo de tomate	tomato juice
zumo de uva	grape juice

SOME COOKING METHODS AND SAUCES

aceite	oil
ahumado	smoked
al ajillo	cooked in oil and garlic
asado	roast, baked
a la brasa/a la barbacoa	barbecued
caliente	hot
carne	meat
poco hecha	rare
mediana	medium
muy hecha	well-done
casero	home-made
cocido	boiled
cocido al vapor	steamed
crudo	raw
en escabeche	marinated in a sweet and sour sauce
escalfado	poached
frío	cold
frito	fried
gratinado	grated
guisado/estofado	braised/stewed
mantequilla	butter
marinado	marinated
a la parrilla	grilled

con perejil	with parsley
a la plancha	'grilled' on the hot plate
rebozado	breaded or fried in batter
relleno	stuffed
a la romana	fried in batter
salsa allioli	oil and garlic sauce
salsa mahonesa	mayonnaise
salsa romesco	sauce of tomatoes, garlic and hot peppers
salsa vinagreta	vinaigrette
con tomates y pimientos verdes	with tomatoes and green peppers
a la vasca	with parsley, garlic and peas

SHOPPING & SERVICES[1]

WHERE TO GO

Which is the best ...?	¿Cuál es el mejor ...?	Kwal es el me-hor
Can you recommend a ...?	¿Puede usted recomendarme ...?	Pwe-de oos-te re-ko-men-dar-me
Where is the market?	¿Dónde está el mercado?	Don-de es-ta el mair-ka-do
Is there a market every day?	¿Hay mercado todos los días?	Eye mair-ka-do to-dos los dee-as
Where's the nearest chemist?	¿Dónde está la farmacia más próxima?	Don-de es-ta la far-ma-thee-a mas pro-see-ma
Where can I buy ...?	¿Dónde puedo comprar ...?	Don-de pwe-do kom-prar

1. Shops are open from 9.00 or 9.30 a.m. to 1.30 p.m., and from 3.00 or 4.00 p.m. to 7.30 p.m.

| When are the shops open? | ¿Cuándo abren las tiendas? | Kwan-do a-bren las tee-en-das |

SHOPS AND SERVICES

antique shop	la tienda de antigüedades	tee-en-da de an-tee-gwe-da-des
baker	la panadería	pa-na-dair-ee-a
bank	el banco	bank-ko
barber (see p. 127)	la barbería	bar-bair-ee-a
bookshop	la librería	lee-brai-ree-a
builder	el constructor	kons-trook-tor
butcher (see p. 99)	la carnicería	kar-nee-thair-ee-a
cake shop	la pastelería	pas-te-le-ree-a
camping equipment	los utensilios para camping	oo-ten-see-lee-os para kam-peeng
carpenter	el carpintero	kar-peen-tair-o
chemist (see p. 119)	la farmacia	far-ma-thee-a
confectioner	la pastelería	pas-te-le-ree-a
dairy	la lechería	le-chair-ee-a
decorator/painter	el decorador/pintor	de-ko-ra-dor/peen-tor
delicatessen (see p. 96)	la mantequería	man-te-kair-ee-a
dentist (see p. 184)	el dentista	den-tees-ta
department store (see p. 113)	los almacenes	alma-then-es
doctor (see p. 174)	el médico	me-dee-ko

dry cleaner (see p. 131)	**la tintorería**	teen-tor-air-**ee**-a
electrician	**el electricista**	e-lek-tree-**thees**-ta
electrical appliances	**los electrodomésticos**	e-lek-tro-do-**mes**-tee-kos
fishmonger (see pp. 98 and 126)	**la pescadería**	pes-ka-dair-**ee**-a
florist	**la floristería**	flo-ris-tair-**ee**-a
gardener	**el jardinero**	har-dee-ne-ro
greengrocer (see pp. 102 and 105)	**la verdulería**	bair-doo-lair-**ee**-a
grocer (see pp. 104 and 106)	**alimentación/ comestibles/ ultramarinos**	a-lee-men-ta-**thyon**/ko-mes-tee-bles/ ool-tra-ma-ree-nos
haberdashery	**la mercería**	mair-thair-**ee**-a
hairdresser (see p. 127)	**la peluquería**	pe-loo-kair-**ee**-a
hardware shop (see p. 129)	**la ferretería**	fer-re-te-**ree**-a
ironmonger	**la cerrajería/ ferretería**	ther-ra-he-**ree**-a/fer-re-te-**ree**-a
jeweller	**la joyería**	hoy-air-**ee**-a
launderette/laundry (see p. 131)	**la lavandería**	la-ban-dair-**ee**-a
market	**el mercado**	mair-ka-do
newsagent (see p. 133)	**el quiosco de periódicos**	kyos-ko de pe-ree-o-dee-kos
notary	**el notario**	no-ta-ree-o
optician	**el óptico**	**op**-tee-ko
pastry shop	**la repostería/ pastelería**	re-pos-tair-**ee**-a/pas-te-le-**ree**-a

photographer (see p. 135)	**el fotógrafo**	fo-**to**-gra-fo
plasterer	**el enlucidor/yesero**	en-loo-thee-dor/ye-se-ro
plumber	**el fontanero**	fon-ta-ne-ro
police	**la policía**	po-lee-**thee**-a
post office	**correos**	ko-rre-os
shoe repairer	**el zapatero**	tha-pa-tair-oh
shoe shop (see pp. 123 and 125)	**la zapatería**	tha-pa-tair-**ee**-a
sports shop	**la tienda de deportes**	tee-en-da de de-por-tes
stationer	**la papelería**	pa-pe-le-**ree**-a
supermarket	**el supermercado**	soo-per-mair-ka-do
sweet shop	**la confitería**	kon-fee-te-**ree**-a
tobacconist (see p. 138)	**el estanco**	es-tan-ko
toy shop	**la juguetería/tienda de juguetes**	hoo-ge-tair-**ee**-a/tee-en-da de hoo-ge-tes
travel agent	**la agencia de viajes**	a-**hen**-thee-a de bee-a-hes
wine merchant	**la bodega**	bo-de-ga

IN THE SHOP

self-service	*autoservicio	ow-to-sair-bee-thee-o
sale (clearance)	*saldo/liquidación	sal-do/lee-kee-da-**thyon**
cash desk	*caja	ka-ha
shop assistant	el dependiente	de-pen-dee-en-te

shop assistant	**el dependiente**	de-pen-dee-en-te
manager	**el encargado/el jefe**	en-kar-ga-do/el he-fe
Can I help you?	*¿**Qué desea?**	Ke de-se-a
I want to buy ...	**Quiero comprar ...**	Kee-e-ro kom-prar
Do you sell ...?	**¿Venden ustedes ...?**	Ben den oos-te-des
I'm just looking around	**Voy a dar una vuelta**	Boy a dar oon-a bwel-ta
I don't want to buy anything now	**Por el momento no voy a comprar nada**	Por el mo-men-to no boy a kom-prar na-da
Could you show me ...?	**¿Puede enseñarme ...?**	Pwe-de en-sai-nyar-me
I don't like this	**Esto no me gusta**	Es-to no me goos-ta
I'll have this	**Me quedo esto**	Me ke-do es-to
We do not have that	*No tenemos eso	No te-ne-mos eso
You'll find them in the ... department	*Eso lo encontrará en el departamento de ...	E-so lo en-kon-tra-ra en el de-par-ta-men-to de
We've sold out but we'll have more tomorrow	*No tenemos ahora pero tendremos mañana	No te-ne-mos a-ora pe-ro ten-dre-mos ma-nya-na
Can I order one?	**¿Puedo encargar uno?**	Pwe-do en-kar-gar oon-o
Anything else?	*¿**Algo más?**	Al-go mas
That will be all	**Esto es todo**	Es-to es to-do
Shall we send it, or will you take it with you?	*¿**Se lo mandamos, o lo lleva usted?**	Se lo man-da-mos o lo llye-ba oos-te
I will take it with me	**Lo llevo**	Lo llye-bo
Please send them to ...	**Mándenlos a ...**	**Man**-den-los a ...

CHOOSING

I want something in leather/green	Quiero algo en piel/verde	Kee-e-ro al-go en pee-el/bair-de
I need it to match this	Quiero que combine con esto	Kee-e-ro ke kon-bee-ne kon es-to
I like the colour but not the style	Me gusta el color pero no el estilo	Me goo-sta el ko-lor pe-ro no el es-tee-lo
I want a darker/lighter shade	Quiero un tono más oscuro/más claro	Kee-e-ro oon to-no mas os-koo-ro/mas kla-ro
I need something warmer/thinner	Necesito algo más caliente/más ligero	Ne-the-see-to al-go mas ka-lee-en-te/mas lee-he-ro
Do you have one in another colour/size?	¿Lo tienen en otro color/talla?	Lo tee-e-nen en ot-ro ko-lor/ta-llya
Have you anything better/cheaper?	¿Tienen algo mejor/más barato?	Tee-en-en al-go me-hor/mas ba-ra-to
That is too much	Es demasiado	Es de-ma-see-a-do
Is there a mirror?	¿Hay un espejo?	Ay oon es-pe-ho
What size is this?	¿Qué talla es ésta?	Ke ta-llya es es-ta
Have you a larger/smaller one?	¿Tienen mayor/más pequeña?	Tee-en-en ma-yor/mas pe-ke-nya
I take size[1] ...	Uso la talla ...	Oo-so la ta-llya
The English/American size is ...	La talla inglesa/americana es ...	La ta-llya een-gle-sa/ame-ree-ka-na es
Can I try it on?	¿Puedo probármelo?	Pwe-do pro-bar-me-lo

1. See CLOTHING SIZES (p. 124).

It's too	**Es demasiado**	Es de-ma-see-a-do
short	**corto**	kor-to
long	**largo**	lar-go
tight	**estrecho**	es-tre-cho
loose	**ancho**	an-cho
Could I see that one, please?	**¿Puedo ver ese, por favor?**	Pwe-do bair ese, por fa-bor
Is it colour-fast?	**¿Está destinta?**	Es-ta des-teen-ta
Is it machine-washable?	**¿Se puede lavar en la lavadora?**	Se pwe-de la-bar en la la-ba-do-ra
Will it shrink?	**¿Encogerá?**	En-ko-he-ra
Is it handmade?	**¿Está hecho a mano?**	Es-ta e-cho a ma-no
For how long is it guaranteed?	**¿Por cuánto tiempo está garantizado?**	Por kwan-to tee-em-po es-ta ga-ran-tee-tha-do
What is it made of?	**¿De qué es?/¿de qué está hecho?**	De ke es?/de ke es-ta e-cho

MATERIALS

cotton	**el algodón**	al-go-don
lace	**el encaje**	en-ka-he
leather	**el cuero**	kwe-ro
linen	**lino**	lee-no
plastic	**el plástico**	plas-tee-ko
silk	**la seda**	se-da
suede	**el ante**	an-te
synthetic	**sintético**	seen-te-tee-ko
wool	**la lana**	la-na

COLOURS

beige	**beige**	bezh
black	**negro**	ne-gro
blue	**azul**	a-thool
brown	**marrón**	mar-ron
cream	**crema**	kre-ma
gold	**oro**	or-o
green	**verde**	bair-de
grey	**gris**	grees
mauve	**morado**	mo-ra-do
orange	**naranja**	na-ran-ha
pink	**rosa**	ro-sa
purple	**morado**	mo-ra-do
red	**rojo**	ro-ho
silver	**plata**	pla-ta
white	**blanco**	blan-ko
yellow	**amarillo**	a-ma-ree-llyo

COMPLAINTS

I want to see the manager	**Quiero hablar con el gerente**	Kee-ero ab-lar kon el he-ren-te
I bought this yesterday	**Compré esto ayer**	Kom-pre es-to a-yair
It doesn't work/fit	**No funciona/sirve**	No foon-thee-ona/seer-be

This is	**Está**	Es-**ta**
dirty	**sucio**	soo-thyo
stained	**manchado**	man-cha-do
torn	**roto**	ro-to
broken	**estropeado**	es-tro-pe-ado
cracked	**rajado**	ra-ha-do
bad	**en malas condiciones**	en-mal-as kon-dee-thee-o-nes

I want to return this	**Quiero devolver esto**	Kee-e-ro de-bol-bair es-to
Will you change it, please?	**¿Pueden cambiármelo?**	Pwe-den kam-bee-**ar**-me-lo
Will you refund my money?	**¿Pueden devolverme el dinero?**	Pwe-den de-bol-bair-me el dee-ne-ro
The receipt	**El recibo/la factura**	El re-thee-bo/la fak-too-ra

PAYING

How much is this?	**¿Cuánto es esto?**	Kwan-to es es-to
That's ... pesetas, please	***Son ... pesetas**	Son ... pe-se-tas
They are ... pesetas each	***Son ... pesetas cada uno**	Son ... pe-se-tas ka-da oon-o
How much does that come to?	**¿Cuánto es?**	Kwan-to es
That will be ...	***Importará/serán ...**	Eem-por-ta-**ra**/se-ran

Can I pay with English/American currency?	¿Puedo pagar con dinero inglés/ americano?	Pwe-do pa-gar kon dee-nair-o een-**gles**/a-meir-ee-ka-no
Do you take credit-cards/travellers' cheques?	¿Aceptan tarjetas de crédito/cheques de viajero?	Athep-tan tar-he-tas de kre-dee-to/che-kes de bya-hair-o
Do you give any discount?	¿Hacen descuento?	A-then des-koo-en-to
Do I have to pay VAT?	¿Tengo que pagar IVA?	Ten-go ke pa-gar ee-ba
Please pay the cashier	*Pague en la caja	Pa-ge en la ka-ha
May I have a receipt, please	Quiero un recibo, por favor	Kee-e-ro oon re-thee-bo por fa-bor
You've given me the wrong change	Creo que el cambio no está bien	Kreo ke el cam-byo no es-ta bee-en

CHEMIST[1]

Can you prepare this prescription for me, please?	¿Pueden hacerme esta receta, por favor?	Pwe-den a-thair-me es-ta re-the-ta por fa-bor
When will it be ready?	¿Cuándo estará listo?	Kwan-do es-ta-**ra** lees-to
Have you a small first-aid kit?	¿Tienen un pequeño botiquín de urgencia?	Tee-e-nen oon pe-ke-nyo bo-tee-**keen** de oor-hen-thee-a
I want some aspirin/ sun cream (for children)	Quiero aspirinas/ crema para el sol (para niños)	Kee-e-ro as-pee-ree-nas/kre-ma pa-ra el sol (pa-ra nee-nyos)

1. See also AT THE DOCTOR'S (p. 174).

I want	Quiero	Kee-e-ro
a mosquito repellent	algo contra los mosquitos	al-go kon-tra los mos-kee-tos
an antiseptic cream	una crema antiséptica	oo-na kre-ma an-tee-sep-tee-ka
a disinfectant	un desinfectante	oon de-seen-fek-tan-te
a mouthwash	un enjuague bucal	oon en-hoo-a-gwe boo-kal
some nose drops	gotas nasales	go-tas na-sa-les
throat lozenges	pastillas para la garganta	pas-tee-llyas pa-ra la gar-gan-ta
stomach pills	pastillas para el estómago	pas-tee-llyas pa-ra el es-to-ma-go
I need something for	Necesito algo para	Ne-the-see-to al-go pa-ra
constipation	el estreñimiento	el es-tre-nyee-mee-en-to
diarrhoea	la diarrea	la dee-a-rre-a
indigestion	la indigestión	la een-dee-hes-tyon
sunburn	las quemaduras del sol	las ke-ma-doo-ras del sol
Do you	¿Venden	Ben-den
sell contraceptives?	anticonceptivos?	an-tee-kon-cep-tee-bos
cotton wool?	algodón?	al-go-don
sanitary towels?	compresas?	kom-pre-sas
tampons?	tampones?	tam-po-nes
I need something for	Necesito algo para	Ne-the-see-to al-go pa-ra
insect bites	las picaduras de insectos	las pee-ka-doo-ras de een-sek-tos
travel sickness	el mareo	el ma-re-o
a hangover	la resaca	la re-sa-ka

TOILET ARTICLES

A packet of razor blades, please	**Un paquete de cuchillas de afeitar, por favor**	Oon pa-ke-te de koo-chee-llyas de afay-tar por fa-bor
How much is this after-shave lotion?	**¿Cuánto cuesta esta loción para el afeitado?**	Kwan-to kwes-ta es-ta lo-**thyon** pa-ra el afay-ta-do
A tube of toothpaste, please	**Un tubo de pasta de dientes/un dentífrico, por favor**	Oon too-bo de pas-ta de dee-en-tes/oon den-tee-free-ko por fa-bor
A box of paper handkerchiefs/a roll of toilet paper, please	**Una caja de pañuelos de papel/un rollo de papel higiénico, por favor**	Oon-a ka-ha de pa-nwe-los de pa-pel/oon ro-llyo de pa-pel ee-hee-e-nee-ko, por fa-bor
I'd like some cleansing cream/ lotion	**Quiero crema/loción limpiadora**	Kee-e-ro kre-ma/lo-**thyon** leem-pee-a-do-ra
hair conditioner	**suavizante para el pelo**	soo-a-bee-than-te pa-ra el pe-lo
hand cream	**crema de manos**	kre-ma de ma-nos
lipsalve	**crema de cacao**	kre-ma de ka-ka-o
moisturizer	**crema hidratante**	kre-ma ee-dra-tan-te
I want some eau-de-cologne/perfume, please	**Un frasco de colonia/perfume, por favor**	Oon fras-ko de ko-lo-nee-a/pair-foo-me por fa-bor
May I try it?	**¿Puedo probarlo?**	Pwe-do pro-bar-lo

| A shampoo for dry/greasy hair, please | Champú para pelo seco/grasiento, por favor | Cham-poo pa-ra pe-lo se-ko/gra-see-en-to por fa-bor |
| Do you have any suntan oil/cream? | ¿Tienen aceite solar/crema solar? | Tee-en-en a-thay-te so-lar/kre-ma solar |

CLOTHES AND SHOES[1]

I want a hat/sunhat	Quiero un sombrero/sombrero para el sol	Kee-er-o oon som-brair-o/som-brair-o pa-ra el sol
I'd like a pair of gloves shoes sandals	Quiero un par de guantes zapatos sandalias	Kee-er-o oon par de gwan-tes tha-pa-tos sand-a-lee-as
May I look at some dresses, please?	Quiero ver vestidos	Kee-ero-o bair best-ee-dos
I like the one in the window	Me gusta el del escaparate	Me goos-ta el del es-ka-pa-ra-te
May I try this?	¿Puedo probarme éste?	Pwe-do pro-bar-me es-te
This doesn't fit	Esto no me vale	Es-to no me ba-le
I don't know the size	No sé el tamaño	No se el ta-ma-nyo
Can you measure me?	¿Me puede medir?	Me pwe-de me-deer
It's for a 3-year-old boy/girl	Es para un niño/una niña de tres años	Es pa-ra oon nee-nyo/oo-na nee-nya de tres an-yos

1. For sizes see p. 124

Where are beach clothes?	¿Dónde están los trajes de playa?	Don-de es-**tan** los tra-hes de pla-ya
Where can I find socks/stockings?	¿Dónde hay calcetines/medias?	Don-de eye kal-the-tee-nes/me-dee-as
I am looking for	Busco	Boos-ko
a blouse	blusas	bloo-sas
a bra	sujetadores	soo-he-ta-do-res
trousers	pantalones	pan-ta-lo-nes
a jacket	chaquetas	cha-ke-tas
a sweater	prendas de punto	pren-das-de poon-to
I need	Necesito	Ne-the-see-to
a coat	un abrigo	oon a-bree-go
a raincoat	un impermeable	oon een-pair-me-a-ble
a hat	un sombrero	oon som-brair-o
Do you sell	¿Venden	Ben-den
buttons?	botones?	bo-to-nes
elastic?	goma?	go-ma
zips?	cremalleras?	kra-ma-llye-ras
I want a short/long-sleeved shirt, collar size …	Quiero una camisa de manga corta/larga, medida de cuello …	Kee-er-o oon-a ka-mee-sa de man-ga kor-ta/lar-ga me-dee-da de kwe-llyo
I need a pair of walking shoes with small heels	Un par de zapatos cómodos de tacón plano	Oon par de tha-pa-tos **ko**-mo-dos de ta-**kon** pla-no
These heels are too high/too low	Este tacón es demasiado alto/bajo	Es-te ta-**kon** es de-ma-see-a-do/al-to ba-ho

CLOTHING SIZES[1]

WOMEN'S DRESSES, ETC

British	10	12	14	16	18	20
American	8	10	12	14	16	18
Continental	30	32	34	36	38	40

MEN'S SUITS

British and American	36	38	40	42	44	46
Continental	46	48	50	52	54	56

MEN'S SHIRTS

British and American	14	$14\frac{1}{2}$	15	$15\frac{1}{2}$	16	$16\frac{1}{2}$	17
Continental	36	37	38	39	41	42	43

WAIST, CHEST/BUST AND HIPS

Inches	28	30	32	34	36	38	40
Centimetres	71	76	81	87	92	97	102
Inches	42	44	46	48	50	52	54
Centimetres	107	112	117	122	127	132	137

---

1. This table is only intended as a rough guide, since sizes vary from manufacturer to manufacturer.

STOCKINGS

British and American	8	8½	9	9½	10	10½	11
Continental	0	1	2	3	4	5	6

SOCKS

British and American	9½	10	10½	11	11½
Continental	38–39	39–40	40–41	41–42	42–43

SHOES

British	1	2	3	4	5	6	7	8	9	10	11	12
American	2½	3½	4½	5½	6½	7½	8½	9½	10½	11½	12½	13½
Continental	33	34–5	36	37	38	39–40	41	42	43	44	45	46

FOOD[1]

Give me a kilo/half a kilo of ..., please	Un kilo/medio kilo de ..., por favor	Oon kee-lo/me-dee-o kee-lo de ... por fa-bor
100 grammes of sweets/chocolates	Cien gramos de caramelos/ bombones	Thee-en gra-mos de ka-ra-me-los/bom-bo-nes
A bottle/litre	Una botella/un litro de leche	Oon-a bo-te-llya/oon lee-tro
of milk		de le-che
of wine	de vino	de bee-no
of beer	de cerveza	de thair-be-tha

1. See also the various MENU sections (p. 96 ff.) and WEIGHTS AND MEASURES (p. 198).

Is there anything back on the bottle?	¿Devuelven algo por la botella?	De-bwel-ben al-go por la bo-te-llya
I want a jar a can packet of	Quiero un tarro una lata un paquete de ...	Kee-e-ro oon tar-ro oon-a la-ta oon pa-ke-te de
... slices of ham please	... cortadas de jamón por favor	kor-ta-das de ha-**mon** por fa-bor
Do you sell frozen foods?	¿Venden alimentos congelados?	Ben-den a-lee-men-tos kon-he-la-dos
Is it fresh or frozen?	¿Es fresco o congelado?	Es fres-ko o kon-he-la-do
These pears are very hard/soft	Estas peras están muy duras/blandas	Es-tas pe-ras es-**tan** mw-ee doo-ras/blan-das
Is it fresh?	¿Está fresco?	Es-ta fres-ko
Are they ripe?	¿Están maduros?	Es-tan ma-doo-ros
This is bad	Está malo	Es-ta ma-lo
A loaf of bread, please[1]	Un pan, por favor	Oon pan por fa-bor
How much a kilo/a bottle?	¿Cuánto cuesta el kilo/la botella?	Kwa-nto koo-es-ta el kee-lo/la bo-te-llya
Will you mince it?	¿Me lo puede picar?	Me lo pw-e-de pee-kar
Will you bone it?	¿Me quita el hueso?	Me kee-ta el oo-e-so
Will you clean the fish?	¿Me limpia el pescado?	Me leen-pee-a el pes-ka-do

1. Spanish bread: **un pan de kilo (medio kilo)** – a loaf weighing 1 kilo ($\frac{1}{2}$ kilo); **un pan de barra** – a French loaf; **bollos/panecilos** – rolls; **un pan de molde** – English loaf.

Leave/take off the head	Deje/quite la cabeza	De-he/kee-te la ka-be-tha
Please fillet the fish	¿Me quita la espina del pescado?	Me kee-ta la es-pee-na del pes-ka-do
I'll take the bones	Me llevo los huesos	Me llye-bo los oo-e-sos
Is there any shellfish?	¿Tiene mariscos?	Tee-e-ne ma-rees-kos
Shall I help myself?	¿Me sirvo yo?	Me seer-bo yo

HAIRDRESSER AND BARBER

May I make an appointment for this morning/tomorrow afternoon?	¿Pueden darme hora para esta mañana/para mañana por la tarde?	Pwe-den dar-me o-ra pa-ra es-ta ma-nya-na/pa-ra ma-nya-na por la tar-de
What time?	¿A qué hora?	A ke o-ra
I want my hair cut/trimmed	Quiero cortarme el pelo/cortarme las puntas	Kee-e-ro kor-tar-me el pe-lo/kor-tar-me las poon-tas
No shorter	No más corto	No mas kor-to
Not too short at the sides	No demasiado corto de los lados	No de-ma-see-a-do kor-to de los la-dos
I'll have it shorter at the back/on top	Más corto por atrás/por arriba	Mas kor-to por a-tras/por ar-ree-ba
My hair is oily/dry	Tengo el pelo grasiento/seco	ten-go el pe-lo gra-see-en-to/se-ko
I want a shampoo	Quiero que me laven la cabeza	Kee-e-ro ke me la-ben la ka-be-tha

Please use conditioner	Por favor quiero suavizante	Por fa-bor kee-e-ro soo-a-bee-than-te
I want my hair washed, styled and blow-dried	Quiero lavar y marcar (secado a mano)	Kee-e-ro la-bar ee mar-kar (se-ka-do a ma-no)
I want my hair washed and set	Quiero que me laven y me peinen	Kee-e-ro ke me la-ben ee me pe-ee-nen
Please set it without rollers/on large/small rollers	Sin rulos, por favor/ con rulos grandes/pequeños, por favor	Seen roo-los, por fa-bor/ kon roo-los gran-des/ pe-ke-nyos por fa-bor
I want a perm	Quiero una permanente	Kee-e-ro oo-na pair-ma-nen-te
Please do not use any hairspray	No me ponga laca	No me pon-ga la-ka
I want a colour rinse	Quiero un reflejo	Kee-e-ro oon re-fle-ho
I'd like to see a colour chart	¿Puedo ver los colores?	Pwe-do bair los ko-lo-res
I want a darker/lighter shade	Quiero un tono más oscuro/claro	Kee-e-ro oon to-no mas os-koo-ro/kla-ro
The water is too cold	El agua está demasiado fría	El a-gwa el-ta de-ma-see-a-do free-a
The dryer is too hot	El secador calienta demasiado	El se-ka-dor ka-lee-en-ta de-ma-see-a-do
Thank you, I like it very much	Está muy bien	Es-ta mwe bee-en
I want a shave/ manicure, please	¿Pueden afeitarme/ hacerme la manicura, por favor?	Pwe-den a-fay-tar-me/a-thair-me la ma-nee-koo-ra por fa-bor

| Please trim my beard/ my moustache | Córteme un poco la barba/el bigote | Kor-te-me oon po-ko la bar-ba/el bee-gote |
| That's fine | Así está bien | A-see es-ta bee-en |

HARDWARE[1]

Where is the camping equipment?	¿Utensilios de camping, por favor?	Oo-ten-see-lee-os de kam-peeng por fa-bor
Do you have a battery for this?	¿Tienen pilas para esto?	Tee-e-nen pee-las pa-ra es-to
Where can I get butane gas/paraffin?	¿Dónde se puede comprar butano/ parafina?	Don-de se pwe-de kom-prar boo-ta-no/pa-ra-fee-na
I need a bottle-opener a tin-opener corkscrew	Necesito un abre-botellas un abrelatas un sacacorchos	Ne-the-see-to oon a-bre-bo-te-llyas oon a-bre-la-tas oon sa-ka-kor-chos
A small/large screwdriver	Un destornillador pequeño/grande	Oon des-tor-nee-llyador/pe-ke-nyo/gran-de
I'd like some candles/ matches	Velas/cerillas, por favor	Be-las/thair-ee-llyas por fa-bor
I want a torch a knife a pair of scissors	Quiero una linterna un cuchillo unas tijeras	Kee-e-ro oon-a leen-ter-na oon koo-chee-llyo oon-as tee-hair-as
Do you sell string/ rope?	¿Venden cuerda/ soga?	Ben-den koo-er-da/so-ga

1. See also CAMPING (p. 63) and RENTING OR OWNING A PLACE (p. 68).

Where can I find washing-up liquid/scouring powder?	¿Dónde puedo comprar líquido lavavajillas/polvos de fregar?	Don-de pwe-do kom-prar lee-kee-do laba-ba-hee-llyas/pol-bos de frai-gar
Do you have dishcloths/brushes?	¿Tienen paños de cocina/cepillos?	Tee-e-nen pa-nyos de ko-thee-na/the-pee-llyos
I need	Necesito	Ne-the-see-to
a groundsheet	una lona impermeable	oon-a lo-na een-pair-me-a-ble
a bucket	un cubo	oon koo-bo
a frying pan	una sartén	oon-a sar-ten
I want to buy a barbecue	Quiero comprar una barbacoa	Kee-e-ro kom-prar oo-na bar-ba-ko-a
Do you sell charcoal?	¿Venden carbón?	Ben-den kar-bon
adaptor	el adaptador	a-dap-ta-dor
basket	la cesta	thes-ta
duster	la bayeta polvo	ba-lye-ta pol-bo
electrical flex	el cordón flex	kor-don flex
extension lead	el cordón/cable de extensión	kor-don/ka-ble de es-ten-syon
fuse	el fusible	foo-see-ble
fuse wire	el plomo fusible	plo-mo foo-see-ble
insulating tape	la cinta aislante	theen-ta a-ees-lan-te
lightbulb	la bombilla	bomb-bee-llya
penknife	la navaja	na-ba-ha
plug (bath)	el tapón del baño	ta-pon del ba-nyo
plug (electric)	el enchufe	en-choo-fe

LAUNDRY AND DRY CLEANING

Where is the nearest laundry/dry cleaner?	**¿Dónde está la lavandería/la tintorería más próxima?**	Don-de es-**ta** la la-ban-dair-ee-a/la teen-to-rair-ee-a mas **pro**-see-ma
I want to have these things washed/cleaned	**Quiero que me laven/limpien esto**	kee-e-ro ke me la-ben/leem-pee-en es-to
Can you get this stain out?	**¿Se quitará esta mancha?**	Se kee-ta-ra es-ta man-cha
It is coffee wine grease	**Es de café vino grasa**	Es de ka-fe bee-no gra-sa
These stains won't come out	***Estas manchas no se quitan**	Es-tas man-chas no se kee-tan
It only needs to be pressed	**Sólo necesita plancharse**	So-lo ne-the-see-ta plan-char-se
This is torn; can you mend it?	**Esto está roto ¿pueden cosérmelo?**	Es-to es-ta ro-to pwe-den ko-sair-me-lo
There's a button missing	**Me falta un botón**	Me-fal-ta oon bo-**ton**
Will you sew on another one, please?	**¿Pueden ponerme otro?**	Pwe-den po-nair-me o-tro
When will they be ready?	**¿Cuándo estarán?**	Kwan-do es-ta-ran

I need them by this evening/tomorrow	**Los necesito para esta noche/para mañana**	Los ne-the-see-to pa-ra es-ta no-che/pa-ra ma-nya-na
Call back at 5 o'clock	***Vuelva a las cinco**	Bwel-ba a las theen-ko
We can't do it before Thursday	***No podemos hacerlo antes del jueves**	No pode-mos a-thair-lo an-tes del hoo-e-bes
It will take three days	***Estará dentro de tres días**	Es-ta-ra den-tro de tres dee-as
This isn't mine	**Esto no es mío**	Es-to no es mee-o
I've lost my ticket	**He perdido mi recibo**	E pair-dee-do mee re-thee-bo

HOUSEHOLD LAUNDRY

bath towel	**la toalla de baño**	to-a-llya de ba-nyo
blanket	**la manta**	man-ta
napkin	**el pañal/la servilleta**	pa-nyal/sair-bee-llye-ta
pillow case	**el almohadón**	al-mo-a-don
sheet	**la sábana**	sa-ba-na
table cloth	**el mantel**	man-tel
tea towel	**el paño cocina**	pa-nyo ko-thee-na

NEWSPAPERS, BOOKS AND WRITING MATERIALS

Do you sell English/American newspapers?	**¿Venden periódicos ingleses/americanos?**	Ben-den pe-ree-o-dee-kos een-gle-ses/a-mer-ee-ka-nos
Can you get ... newspaper/magazine for me?	**¿Pueden proporcionarme el diario .../la revista ...?**	Pwe-den pro-por-thyo-nar-me el dee-a-ree-o .../la re-bees-ta
Where can I get the ...?	**¿Dónde puedo comprar ...?**	Don-de pwe-do kom-prar
I want a map of the city/a road map	**Quiero un mapa de la ciudad/de carreteras**	kee-e-ro oon ma-pa de la thee-oo-dad/de kar-re-te-ras
Is there an entertainment/amusements guide?	**¿Hay una cartelera?**	Eye oon-a kar-te-le-ra
Do you have any English books?	**¿Tienen libros ingleses?**	Tee-e-nen lee-bros enn-gle-ses
Have you any books by ...?	**¿Tienen algún libro de ...?**	Tee-e-nen al-**goon** lee-bro de
I want some picture postcards	**Quiero unas tarjetas postales de vistas**	Kee-e-ro oon-as tar-he-tas pos-ta-les de bees-tas
Do you sell souvenirs/toys?	**¿Venden objetos de recuerdo/alguna clase de juguetes?**	Ben-den ob-he-tos de re-koo-air-do/al-goo-na kla-se de hoo-ge-tes
ballpoint	**el bolígrafo**	el bol-ee-gra-fo

calculator	**la calculadora**	kal-koo-la-do-ra
card	**la tarjeta**	tar-he-ta
crayon	**la tiza**	la tee-tha
dictionary	**el diccionario**	dee-thee-o-na-ree-o
drawing paper	**el papel para dibujar**	pa-pel pa-ra dee-boo-har
drawing pins	**las chinchetas**	las cheen-che-tas
envelope	**el sobre**	el so-bre
felt-tip pen	**el rotulador**	el ro-too-la-dor
file	**la carpeta**	la kar-pe-ta
glue	**el pegamín**	el pe-ga-meen
guide book	**la guía de la ciudad**	**gee**-a de la thee-oo-dad
ink	**la tinta**	la teen-ta
label	**la etiqueta**	la e-tee-ke-ta
notebook	**el bloc/el cuaderno**	blok/koo-a-der-no
paperclip	**el sujeta papeles**	soo-he-ta-pa-pe-les
pen	**la pluma/el bolígrafo**	ploo-ma/bo-**lee**-gra-fo
pen cartridge	**el recambio**	re-kam-bee-o
pencil	**el lápiz**	el **la**-peeth
pencil sharpener	**el sacapuntas**	sa-ka-poon-tas
postcard	**la tarjeta postal**	tar-he-ta pos-tal
rubber	**la goma**	go-ma
sellotape	**el papel celo**	pa-pel the-lo
string	**la cuerda**	la koo-air-da
writing paper	**el papel de cartas**	el pa-pel de kar-tas

OPTICIAN

I have broken my glasses. Can you repair them?	**Se me han roto los lentes. ¿Me los puede arreglar?**	Se me an ro-to los lentes. Me los pwe-de arreg-lar
Can you give me a new pair of glasses with the same prescription?	**¿Podría hacerme unos lentes nuevos con la misma receta?**	Po-dree-a a-thair-me oo-n os len-tes nwe-bos kon la mees-ma re-the-ta
I have difficulty with reading	**Tengo dificultades para leer**	Ten-go dee-fee-kool-ta-des pa-ra lay-er
I have difficulty with long distance vision	**No veo bien de lejos**	No be-o bee-en de le-hos
Please test my eyes	**Por favor necesito que me revise la vista**	Por fa-bor ne-the-see-to ke me re-be-se la bees-ta
I have lost one of my contact lenses	**He perdido una de mis lentillas**	Ai pair-dee-do oo-na de mees len-tee-llyas
I should like to have contact lenses	**Quiero un par de lentillas**	Kee-e-ro oon par de len-tee-llyas
I am short-sighted	**Soy corto de vista**	Soy kor-to de bees-ta
I am long-sighted	**Tengo la vista larga**	Ten-go la bees-ta lar-ga

PHOTOGRAPHY

I want to buy a camera	**Quiero una máquina fotográfica**	Kee-e-ro oon-a ma-kee-na fo-to-gra-fee-ka
Have you a film for this camera?	**¿Tienen carretes para esta máquina?**	Tee-e-nen kar-re-tes pa-ra es-ta ma-kee-na

I want a (fast) colour film/black and white film	Una película (rápida) en color/en blanco y negro	Oon-a pe-lee-koo-la (ra-pee-da) en ko-lor/en blan-ko ee ne-gro
A 100/400/1000 ASA film please	Quiero un carrete de cien/cuatrocientos/mil ASA	Kee-e-ro oon kar-re-te de thee-en/kwa-tro-thee-en-tos/meel a-sa
What is the fastest film you have?	¿Cuál es el carrete de película más rápido?	Kwal es el kar-re-te de pe-lee-koo-la mas ra-pee-do
Would you fit the film in the camera for me, please?	Haga el favor de ponerme el carrete en la máquina	Aga el fa-bor de pon-air-me el kar-re-te en la ma-kee-na
Does the price include processing?	¿Está el revelado incluido?	Es-ta el re-be-la-do een-kloo-ee-do
I'd like this film developed and printed	Quiero revelado y copias de este carrete	Kee-e-ro re-be-la-do ee ko-pee-as de es-te kar-re-te
Can I have a print/enlargement of this negative?	¿Me puede hacer una foto/una ampliación de este negativo?	Me pwe-de a-thair oo-na fo-to/oo-na am-plee-a-thyon de es-te ne-ga-tee-bo
When will it be ready?	¿Cuándo estará?	Kwan-do es-ta-ra
Will it be done tomorrow?	¿Estará mañana?	Es-ta-ra ma-nya-na
Will it be ready by ...?	¿Puede estar para ...?	Pwe-de es-tar pa-ra
My camera's not working. Can you check it/mend it?	Esta máquina no funciona. ¿Pueden revisarla?/¿Pueden arreglármela?	Es-ta ma-kee-na no foon-thee-o-na. Pwe-den re-bee-sar-la/Pwe-den ar-reg-lar-me-la

The film is jammed	**No pasa el carrete**	No pa-sa el ka-re-te
There is something wrong with the flash	**El flash no funciona**	El flash no foon-thee-o-na
battery	**la pila**	pee-la
cine film	**la película de cine**	pe-lee-koo-la de thee-ne
filter	**el filtro**	feel-tro
lens	**el lente**	len-te
lens cap	**la tapa del lente**	ta-pa del len-te
light meter	**el medidor de la luz**	me-dee-dor de la looth
shutter	**el obturador**	ob-too-ra-dor
slide	**la diapositiva**	dee-a-po-see-tee-ba
video camera	**la cámara de video**	ka-ma-ra de bee-de-o

RECORDS AND CASSETTES

Do you have any records/cassettes of local music?	**¿Tiene discos/casettes de música local?**	Tee-e-ne dees-kos/ka-se-tes de **moo-see-ka** lo-kal
Are there any new records by ...?	**¿Hay algún disco nuevo de ...?**	Eye al-**goonw** dees-ko nwe-bo de
Do you sell compact discs?	**¿Vende compact disc?**	Ben-de kom-pakt deesk
Do you sell video cassettes?	**¿Vende casettes de video?**	Ben-de ka-se-tes de bee-de-o

TOBACCONIST[1]

Do you stock English/ American cigarettes?	¿Tienen cigarrillos ingleses/ americanos?	Tee-e-nen thee-gar-ree-llyos een-gles-es/a-mer-ee-ka-nos
Virginia/dark tobacco	Tabaco rubio/negro	Ta-ba-ko roo-bee-o/ neg-ro
I want some filter-tip cigarettes	Un paquete de cigarrillos con filtro	Oon-pa-ke-te de thee-gar-ree-llyos kon feel-tro
cigarettes without filter	cigarrillos sin filtro	thee-gar-ree-llyos seen feel-tro
menthol cigarettes	cigarrillos mentolados	thee-gar-ree-llyos men-to-la-dos
A box of matches, please	Una caja de cerillas/fósforos	Oo-na ka-ha de thair-ree-llyas/fos-for-os
I want to buy a lighter	Quiero comprar un encendedor/ mechero	Kee-e-ro kom-prar oon en-then-de-dor/me-che-ro
Do you sell (lighter) fuel/flints?	¿Tienen cargas de gas/piedras (para el encendedor)?	Tee-e-nen kar-gas de gas/pee-e-dras (pa-ra el en-then-de-dor)
I want a gas refill	Quiero un recambio de gas	Kee-e-ro oon re-kam-bee-o de gas
Do you sell cigarette papers?	¿Tienen papel de fumar?	Tee-e-nen pa-pel de foo-mar

1. Tobacconists also sell postage stamps. **Estancos** are recognized by a sign bearing the Spanish national colours (red, yellow, red).

REPAIRS

This is broken. Can you mend it?	**Esto está estropeado. ¿Puede repararlo?**	Es-to es-ta es-tro-pe-a-do. Pwe-de re-pa-rar-lo
Could you do it while I wait?	**¿Puede hacerlo ahora mismo?**	Pwe-de a-thair-lo a-ora mees-mo
When should I come back for it?	**¿Cuándo puedo recogerlo?**	Kwan-do pwe-do re-ko-hair-lo
I want these shoes soled with leather/heeled with rubber	**Quiero que me pongan mediasuelas de cuero/tacones de goma**	Kee-e-ro ke me pon-gan me-dee-a-soo-e-las de koo-e-ro/ta-ko-nes de go-ma
Can you put on new heels?	**¿Puede ponerme tacones nuevos?**	Pwe-de po-nair-me ta-ko-nes nwe-bos
Can you repair this watch?	**¿Pueden arreglarme este reloj?**	Pwe-den arre-glar-me es-te re-loh
I have broken the glass the strap the spring	**Se me ha roto el cristal la correa el muelle**	Se me a ro-to el krees-tal la ko-re-a el mwe-llye
I have broken my glasses the frames the sides	**Se me han roto las gafas la patilla la montura**	Se me an ro-to las ga-fas la pa-tee-llya la mon-too-ra
How much would a new one cost?	**¿Cuánto costaría una nueva?**	Kwan-to kos-tar-ee-a oon-a nwe-ba
The fastener/clip/chain is broken	**El cierre/el clip/la cadena se ha roto**	El thee-er-re/el kleep/la ka-de-na se a ro-to

The stone is loose	**La piedra está suelta**	La pee-e-dra es-**ta** soo-el-ta
It can't be repaired	*No tiene arreglo	No tee-e-ne ar-re-glo
You need a new one	*Necesita uno nuevo/una nueva	Ne-the-see-ta oo-no nwe-bo/oon-a nwe-ba

POST OFFICE

Where's the main post office?	¿Dónde está la oficina principal de correos?	Don-de es-**ta** la of-ee-thee-na preen-thee-pal de kor-re-os
Where's the nearest post office?	¿Dónde está la oficina de correos más próxima?	Don-de es-**ta** la of-ee-the-na de kor-re-os mas **pro**-see-ma
What time does the post office open/close?	¿A qué hora abren/cierran correos?	A ke o-ra a-bren/thee-ar-an kor-re-os
Where's the post box?	¿Dónde hay un buzón de correos?	Don-de eye oon boo-**thon** de kor-re-os
Which counter do I go to for stamps? telegrams? money orders?	¿Cuál es la ventanilla de los sellos? los telegramas? los giros?	Koo-al es la ben-ta-nee-llya de los se-llyos los te-lai-gra-mas los heer-os

LETTERS AND TELEGRAMS[1]

How much is a postcard abroad/to England?	¿Qué sellos llevan las tarjetas postales para el extranjero/para Inglaterra?	Ke se-llyos llye-ban las tar-he-tas pos-tal-es pa-ra el es-tran-he-ro/pa-ra een-gla-te-rra
What's the airmail to the USA?	¿Qué sellos llevan las cartas por avión para los Estados Unidos?	Ke se-llyos llye-ban las kar-tas por a-bee-on pa-ra los es-ta-dos oon-ee-dos
How much is it to send a letter surface mail?	¿Qué sellos llevan las cartas por correo ordinario?	Ke se-llyos llye-ban las kar-tas por kor-reo or-dee-na-ree-o
It's inland	Es para España	Es pa-ra Es-pa-nya
Give me three ... pesetas stamps	Tres sellos de ... pesetas	Tres se-llyos de ... pe-se-tas
I want to send this letter express	Quiero mandar esta carta urgente	Kee-e-ro man-dar es-ta kar-ta oor-hen-te
I want to register this letter	Quiero certificar esta carta	Kee-e-ro thair-tee-fee-kar es-ta kar-ta
I want to send a parcel	Quiero enviar un paquete	Kee-e-ro en-bee-ar oon pa-ke-te
Where is the poste restante section?	¿Dónde está la lista de correos?	Don-de es-ta la lees-ta de kor-re-os
Are there any letters for me?	¿Hay alguna carta a nombre de ...?	Eye al-goo-na kar-ta a nom-bre de

1. You can buy stamps from a tobacconist's as well as from a post office.

What is your name?	*¿(Cuál es) su nombre, por favor?/¿cómo se llama usted?	(Kwal es) soo nom-bre, por fa-bor/Ko-mo se llya-ma oos-te
Have you any means of identification?	*¿Tiene algo que le identifique?	Tee-e-ne al-go ke le ee-den-tee-fee-ke
Can I send a telex	¿Puedo mandar un télex?	Pwe-do man-dar oon te-les
I want to send a (reply paid) telegram	Quiero mandar un telegrama (con respuesta pagada)	Kee-e-ro man-dar oon te-le-gram-a (kon res-poo-es-ta pa-ga-da)
How much does it cost per word?	¿Cuánto cuesta por palabra?	Kwan-to koo-es-ta por pa-la-bra

TELEPHONING[1]

Where's the nearest phone box?	¿Dónde hay un teléfono público?	Don-de eye oon te-le-fo-no poo-bleek-o
May I use your phone?	¿Puedo usar su teléfono?	Pwe-do oo-sar soo te-le-fo-no
Do you have a telephone directory for ...?	¿Tienen una guía telefónica de ...?	Tee-en-en oon-a gee-a te-le-fo-nee-ka de
I want to make a phone call	Quiero hacer una llamada telefónica	Kee-e-ro a-thair oon-a llya-ma-da te-le-fo-nee-ka

1. There are two kinds of telephone box: **urbanas** for local calls only and **interurbanas** for long-distance calls. You can also telephone from most bars and cafés. There is no link between the **correos** and the **telefónica**, they are separate services, and post offices do not contain telephones.

Please get me ...	Quiero una conferencia con el ...	Kee-e-ro oon-a kon-fair-en-thee-a kon el
What do I dial to get the international operator?	¿Cuál es el número para internacional?	Kwal es el **noo**-me-ro pa-ra een-tair-na-thee-o-nal
I want to telephone to England	Quiero poner una conferencia a Inglaterra	Kee-e-ro po-nair oon-a kon-fair-**en**-thee-a a een-gla-te-ra
What is the code for ...?	¿Cuál es el código para ...?	Kwal es el **ko**-dee-go pa-ra
Could you give me the cost/time and charges afterwards?	¿Puede decirme después cuánto es?	Pwe-de de-theer-me des-poo-**es** kwan-to es
I want to reverse the charges/call collect	Quiero una conferencia a cobro revertido	Kee-e-ro oon-a kon-fair-en-thee-a a ko-bro re-bair-tee-do
I was cut off. Can you reconnect me?	Me han cortado. ¿Puede volverme a poner?	Me an kor-ta-do. Pwe-de bol-bair-me a po-nair
I want extension ...	Quiero la extensión ...	Kee-e-ro la es-ten-see-**on**
May I speak to Señor Alvarez?	El Señor Alvarez, por favor	El Se-nyor Al-bar-eth por fa-bor
Who's speaking?	*¿De parte de quién/quién habla?	De par-te de kee-en/ kee-en ha-bla
Hold the line, please	*No se retire	No se re-tee-re
We'll call you back	*Le llamaremos	Le llya-ma-rai-mos
He's not here	*No está en casa/ aquí	No es-ta en ka-sa/a-kee

He's at ...	*Está ...	Es-ta ...
When will he be back?	¿Cuándo volverá?	Kwan-do bol-bair-a
Will you take a message?	¿Puedo dejarle un recado?	Pwe-do de-har-le oon rai-ka-do
Tell him that ... phoned	Dígale que ha llamado ...	Dee-ga-le ke a llya-ma-do ...
I'll ring again later	Llamaré más tarde	Llya-ma-re mas tar-de
Please ask him to phone me	Dígale que me llame, por favor	Dee-ga-le ke me llya-me por fa-bor
What's your number?	*¿Cuál es su número?	Kwal es soo noo-me-ro
My number is ...	Mi número es ...	Mee noo-me-ro es
I can't hear you	No le oigo bien	No le o-ee-go bee-en
The line is engaged	*Está comunicando	Es-ta ko-moo-nee-kan-do
There's no reply	*No contestan	No kont-es-tan
You have the wrong number	*Tiene el número confundido	Tee-e-ne el noo-me-ro kon-foon-dee-do
The number is out of order	*Ese número está estropeado	E-se noo-me-ro es-ta es-tro-pe-a-do

SIGHTSEEING[1]

Where is the tourist office?	¿Dónde está la oficina de turismo?	Don-de es-**ta** la o-fee-**thee**-na de too-**rees**-mo
What should we see here?	¿Qué hay para ver aquí?	Ke eye pa-ra bair a-**kee**
Is there a map/plan of the places to visit?	¿Hay algún plano de los lugares a visitar?	Eye al-**goon** pla-no de los loo-ga-rees a bee-see-tar
I want a good guide book	Quiero una guía turística buena	Kee-e-ro oon-a **gee**-a too-**rees**-tee-ka boo-e-na
Is there a good sightseeing tour?	¿Hay alguna excursión buena?	Eye al-goo-na es-koor-syon boo-e-na
Does the coach stop at ... hotel?	¿Para el autocar en el hotel ...?	Pa-ra el a-oo-to-kar en el o-tel ...
Is there an excursion to ...?	¿Hay una excursión a ...?	Eye oon-a es-koor-**syon** a ...

1. See also TRAVEL (p. 16) and DIRECTIONS (p. 33).

How long does the tour take?	¿Cuánto dura la excursión?	Kwan-to doo-ra la es-koor-syon
Are there guided tours of the museum?	¿Hay una guía con la excursión del museo?	Eye oon-a gee-a kon la es-koor-syon del moo-se-o
Does the guide speak English?	¿Habla el guía inglés?	A-bla el gee-a een-gles
We don't need a guide	No necesitamos un guía	No ne-the-see-ta-mos oon gee-a
I would prefer to go round alone; is that all right?	Prefiero ir yo solo; ¿se puede hacer?	Pre-fee-e-ro eer yo so-lo; se pwe-de a-thair
How much does the tour cost?	¿Cuánto cuesta la excursión?	Kwan-to kwes-ta la es-koor-syon
Are all admission fees included?	¿Están todas las entradas incluidas?	Es-tan to-das las en-tra-das een-kloo-ee-das
Does it include lunch?	¿Está incluida la comida?	Es-ta een-kloo-ee-da la ko-mee-da

MUSEUMS AND ART GALLERIES

When does the museum open/close?	¿A qué hora abren/cierran el museo?	A ke o-ra a-bren/thee-e-ran el moo-se-o
Is it open every day?	¿Está abierto todos los días?	Es-ta a-bee-er-to to-dos los dee-as
The gallery is closed on Mondays	La galería está cerrada los lunes	La ga-le-ree-a es-ta the-rra-da los loo-nes
How much does it cost?	¿Cuánto cuesta?	Kwan-to kwes-ta

Are there reductions for	¿Hay descuento para	Eye des-koo-en-to pa-ra
children?	los niños?	los nee-nyos
students?	los estudiantes?	los es-too-dee-an-tes
the elderly?	los de la tercera edad?	los de la tair-the-ra e-dad
Are admission fees lower on any special day?	¿Hay precios reducidos en días especiales?	Eye pre-thee-os re-doo-thee-dos en dee-as es-pe-thee-a-les
Admission free	*Entrada gratuita	En-tra-da gra-too-ee-ta
Have you got a ticket?	*¿Tiene Usted entrada?	Tee-e-ne oos-te en-tra-da
Where do I buy a ticket?	¿Dónde compro la entrada?	Don-de kom-pro la en-tra-da
Please leave your bag in the cloakroom	*Por favor dejen los bolsos en el guardarropa	Por fa-bor de-hen los bol-sos en el gwar-dar-ro-pa
It's over there	Está allí	Es-ta a-llyee
Where is the ... collection/exhibition?	¿Dónde está la colección/exposición (de) ...?	Don-de es-ta la ko-lek-thyon/es-po-see-thyon (de)
Can I take photographs?	¿Puedo sacar fotografías?	Pwe-do sa-kar fo-to-gra-fee-as
Can I use a tripod?	¿Puedo utilizar un trípode?	Pwe-do oo-tee-lee-thar oon tree-po-de
Photographs are not allowed	*Prohibido sacar fotos	Pro-ee-bee-do sa-kar fo-tos
I want to buy a catalogue	Quiero comprar un catálogo	Kee-e-ro kom-prar oon ka-ta-lo-go
Will you make photocopies?	¿Hacen fotocopias?	A-then fo-to-ko-pee-as

| Could you make me a transparency of this painting? | ¿Puede sacarme una transparencia de este cuadro? | Pwe-de sa-kar-me oon-a trans-pa-ren-thya de es-te koo-a-dro |
| How long will it take? | ¿Cuánto tiempo tardará? | Kwan-to tee-em-po tar-da-ra |

HISTORICAL SITES

We want to visit ... can we get there by car?	Queremos visitar ... ¿podemos ir en coche?	Ke-rai-mos bee-see-tar ... po-de-mos eer en ko-che
Is there far to walk?	¿Hay que andar mucho?	Eye ke an-dar moo-cho
Is it an easy walk?	¿El camino es fácil?	El ka-mee-no es fa-theel
Is there access for wheelchairs?	¿Se pueden llevar sillas de ruedas?	Se pwe-den llye-bar see-llyas de rwe-das
Is it far to	¿Está lejos	Es-ta le-hos
the aqueduct?	el acueducto?	el a-kwe-dook-to
the castle?	el castillo?	el kas-tee-llyo
the fort?	el fuerte/la fortaleza?	el fwer-te/la for-ta-le-tha
the gate?	la puerta/valla/muralla?	la pwer-ta/ba-llya/moo-ra-llya
the fountain?	la fuente?	la fwen-te
the walls?	las murallas?	las moo-ra-llyas
the fortifications?	las fortificaciones?	las for-tee-fee-ka-thyo-nes
When was it built?	¿Cuándo fue construido?	Kwan-do fwe kons-troo-ee-do
Who built it?	¿Quién lo construyó?	Kee-e-en lo kons-troo-lyo

Where is the old part of the city?	¿Dónde está la parte vieja de la ciudad?	Don-de es-ta la par-te bee-e-ha de la thee-oo-dad
What is the building?	¿Qué es este edificio?	Ke es es-te e-dee-fee-thyo
Where is the house of ...? the church of ...? the cemetery of ...?	¿Dónde está la casa de ...? la iglesia de ...? el cementerio de ...?	Don-de es-ta la ka-sa de ... la ee-gle-see-a de ... el the-men-te-ree-o de ...

GARDENS, PARKS AND ZOOS

Where is the botanical garden/zoo?	¿Dónde está el jardín botánico/zoo?	Don-de es-ta el har-deen bo-ta-nee-ko/thoo
How do I get to the park?	¿Cómo puedo ir hasta el parque?	Ko-mo pwe-do eer as-ta el par-ke
Can we walk there?	¿Podemos ir andando?	Po-de-mos eer an-dan-do
Can we drive through the park?	¿Se puede ir en coche por el parque?	Se pwe-de eer en ko-che por el par-ke
Are the gardens open to the public?	¿Los jardines están abiertos al público?	Los har-dee-nes es-tan a-bee-er-tos al poo-blee-ko
What time do the gardens close?	¿A qué hora cierran los jardines?	A ke o-ra thee-e-rran los har-dee-nes
Is there a plan of the gardens?	¿Hay un plano de los jardines?	Eye oon pla-no de los har-dee-nes

Who designed the gardens?	¿Quién diseñó los jardines?	Kee-en dee-se-nyo los har-dee-nes
Where is the tropical plant house/lake?	¿Dónde está el invernadero/el lago?	Don-de es-ta el een-bair-na-de-ro/el la-go

EXPLORING

I'd like to walk round the old town	Quiero dar una vuelta por la parte vieja	Kee-e-ro dar oon-a bwel-ta por la par-te bee-e-ha
Is there a good street plan showing the buildings?	¿Hay algún plano de los edificios?	Eye al-goon pla-no de los e-dee-fee-thyos
We want to visit the cathedral the fortress	Queremos visitar la catedral el fuerte/el castillo	Ke-rai-mos bee-see-tar la ka-te-dral el fwer-te/el kas-tee-llyo
the library the monastery the palace the ruins	la biblioteca el monasterio el palacio las ruinas	la bee-blee-o-te-ka el mo-nas-te-ree-o el pa-la-thyo las roo-ee-nas
May we walk around the walls?	¿Podemos andar por las murallas?	Po-de-mos an-dar por las moo-ra-llyas
May we go up the tower?	¿Podemos subir a la torre?	Po-de-mos soo-beer a la to-rre
Where is the antiques market/flea market?	¿Dónde está el mercado de antigüedades/el rastro?	Don-de es-ta el mai-ka-do de an-tee-gwe-da-des/el ras-tro

GOING TO CHURCH

Is there	¿Dónde hay	Don-de eye
a Catholic church?	una iglesia católica?	oon-a ee-gle-see-a ka-to-lee-ka
a Protestant church?	una iglesia protestante?	oon-a ee-gle-see-a pro-tes-tan-te
a mosque?	una mezquita?	oon-a meth-kee-ta
a synagogue?	una sinagoga?	oon-a see-na-go-ga
What time is mass/the service?	¿A qué hora hay misa/servicio?	A ke o-ra eye mee-sa/ser-bee-thyo
I'd like to look round the church?	Quiero ver la iglesia	Kee-e-ro bair la ee-gle-see-a
When was the church built?	¿Cuándo se construyó la iglesia?	Kwan-do se kons-troo-yo la ee-gle-see-a
Should women cover their heads?	¿Se tienen que cubrir la cabeza las mujeres?	Se tee-e-nen ke koo-breer la ka-be-tha las moo-he-res

ENTERTAINMENT

Is there an entertainment guide?	¿Hay guía de espectáculos?	Eye **gee**-a de es-pek-ta-koo-los
What's on at the theatre/cinema[1]?	¿Qué hay en los teatros/cines?	Ke eye en los te-a-tros/thee-nes
Is there a concert?	¿Hay algún concierto?	Eye al-**goon** kon-thyair-to
Can you recommend a good ballet/film/musical?	¿Qué ballet/película/revista musical me recomienda?	Ke ba-let/pe-lee-koo-la/re-bees-ta moo-see-kal me re-ko-mee-en-da
Who is directing? conducting? singing?	¿Quién es el director? es el director de la orquesta? canta?	Kee-en es el dee-rek-tor es el dee-rek-tor de la or-kes-ta kan-ta

1. Usually there are two performances daily in theatres and some cinemas. The first (**tarde**) begins at 7.30 or 8 p.m., and the second (**noche**) at 10.30 or 11 p.m. Theatres often have two performances on Sundays, starting at 4.30 p.m. In other cinemas the show goes on continuously, starting at 4.30.

Who is	¿Quién	Kee-en
directing?	es el director?	es el dee-rek-tor
conducting?	es el director de la orquesta?	es el dee-rek-tor de la or-kes-ta
singing?	canta?	kan-ta
I want two seats for tonight	Quiero dos entradas para esta noche	Kee-e-ro dos en-tra-das pa-ra es-ta no-che
Is the matinée sold out?	¿Hay entradas para el matiné?	Eye en-tra-das pa-ra el ma-tee-ne
I'd like seats	Quiero entradas	Kee-e-ro en-tra-das
in the stalls	de butaca	de boo-ta-ka
in the circle	de general	de he-ne-ral
in the gallery	de gallinero	de ga-llyee-ne-ro
The cheapest seats, please	Por favor las entradas más baratas	Por fa-bor las en-tra-das mas ba-ra-tas
I want to book seats for Thursday	Quiero reservar entradas para el jueves	Kee-e-ro re-sair-bar en-tra-das pa-ra el hwe-bes
That performance is sold out	*No hay entradas para esta sesión	No eye en-tra-das pa-ra es-ta se-syon
Are they good seats?	¿Son buenas estas entradas?	Son bwe-nas es-tas en-tra-das
Where are these seats?	¿Dónde están estos asientos?	Don-de es-tan es-tos a-see-en-tos
What time does the performance start?	¿A qué hora empieza la función?	A ke o-ra em-pee-e-tha la foon-thyon
What time does it end?	¿A qué hora termina?	A ke o-ra tair-mee-na
Where is the cloakroom?	¿Dónde está el guardarropa?	Don-de es-ta el gwar-dar-ro-pa
This is your seat	*Este es su asiento	Es-te es soo a-see-en-to

A programme, please	Un programa, por favor	Oon pro-gra-ma por fa-bor
Which is the best nightclub/disco?	¿Cuál es la mejor sala de fiestas/discoteca?	Kwal es la me-hor sa-la de fee-es-tas/dees-ko-te-ka
What time is the floorshow?	¿A qué hora es el espectáculo?	A ke o-ra es el es-pek-ta-koo-lo
Would you like to dance?	¿Quiere bailar?	Kee-e-re ba-ee-lar
Is there a jazz club here?	¿Hay alguna sala/algún club de jazz?	Eye al-goo-na sa-la/al-goon kloob de jazz
Where can we go dancing?	¿Dónde podemos ir a bailar?	Don-de po-de-mos eer a ba-ee-lar

SPORTS & GAMES

Where is the nearest tennis court/golf course?	¿Dónde hay una pista de tenis/un campo de golf?	Don-de eye oo-na pees-ta de te-nees/oon kam-po de golf
What is the charge per game? hour? day?	¿Cuánto vale por partida? hora? día?	Kwan-to ba-le por par-tee-da o-ra dee-a
Is it a club?	¿Hay algún club?	Eye al-**goon** kloob
Do I need temporary membership?	¿Tengo que hacerme socio?	Ten-go ke a-thair-me so-thyo
Where can we go swimming/fishing?	¿Dónde puedo ir a nadar/a pescar?	Don-de pwe-do eer a na-dar/a pes-kar
Can I hire a racket? clubs? fishing tackle?	¿Puedo alquilar una raqueta? palos de golf? una caña de pescar?	Pwe-do al-kee-lar oo-na ra-ke-ta pa-los de golf oo-na ka-nya de pes-kar
Do I need a permit?	¿Necesito permiso/licencia?	Ne-the-see-to per-mee-so/lee-then-thya

Where do I get a permit?	¿Dónde puedo sacar la licencia?	Don-de pe-do sa-kar la lee-then-thya
Can we swim in the river?	¿Podemos nadar en el río?	Po-de-mos na-dar en el ree-o
Is there a swimming pool?	¿Hay piscina?	Eye pees-thee-na
Is it heated?	¿Está climatizada?	Es-ta klee-ma-tee-tha-da
Is there a skating rink?	¿Hay pista de patinaje sobre hielo?	Eye pees-ta de pa-tee-na-he so-bre ee-e-lo
Can I hire skates/ skiing equipment?	¿Puedo alquilar patines/equipo de esquiar?	Pwe-do al-kee-lar pa-tee-nes/e-kee-po de es-kee-ar
Can I take lessons here?	¿Dan lecciones?	Dan le-thyo-nes
I've never skied before	No he esquiado antes	No e es-kee-a-do an-tes
Are there ski runs for beginners?	¿Tienen línea para principiantes?	Tee-e-nen lee-nea pa-ra preen-thee-pee-an-tes
I'd like to go cross-country skiing	Quiero esquiar a campo abierto	Kee-e-ro es-kee-ar a kam-po a-bee-er-to
Are there ski lifts?	¿Hay funiculares?	Eye foo-nee-koo-la-res
We want to go to a football match	Queremos ir a un partido de fútbol	Ke-rai-mos eer a oon par-tee-do de foot-bol
the tennis tournament	un partido de tenis	oon par-tee-do de te-nees
the bullfight	los toros	los to-ros
Can you get us tickets?	¿Nos puede sacar entradas?	Nos pwe-de sa-kar en-tra-das

Are there seats in the grandstand?	¿Tienen entradas de tribuna?	Tee-e-nen en-tra-das de tree-boo-na
How much are the cheapest seats?	¿Cuánto valen las entradas más baratas?	Kwan-to ba-len las en-tra-das mas ba-ra-tas
Are they in the sun or the shade?	¿Son de sol o sombra?	Son de sol o som-bra
Who is playing?	¿Quién juega?	Kee-en hoo-e-ga
When does it start?	¿A qué hora empieza?	A ke o-ra em-pee-etha
Who is winning?	¿Quién gana?	Kee-en ga-na
What is the score?	¿Cómo van?	Ko-mo ban
I'd like to ride	Quiero montar a caballo	Kee-e-ro mon-tar a ka-ba-llyo
Is there a riding stable nearby?	¿Hay escuela hípica cerca?	Eye es-koo-e-la ee-pee-ka thair-ka
Do you give lessons?	¿Dan lecciones?	Dan le-thee-o-nes
I am a good rider	Monto a caballo bien	Mon-to a ka-ba-llyo bee-en
Where is the race course?	¿Dónde está el hipódromo?	Don-de es-ta el ee-po-dro-mo
Which is the favourite?	¿Cuál es el favorito?	Kwal es el fa-bo-ree-to
Who is the jockey?	¿Quién es el jockey?	Kee-en es el ho-kee
... pesetas to win on .../for a place ...	... pesetas apuesta a ganar .../por lugar ...	pe-se-tas a-poo-es-ta a ga-nar/por loo-gar
What are the odds?	¿Qué porcentaje hay?	Ke por-then-ta-he eye
Do you play cards?	¿Juega a las cartas?	Hwe-ga a las kar-tas

Would you like a game of chess?	¿Quiere que juguemos al ajedrez?	Kee-e-re ke hoo-ge-mos al a-he-dreth
I'd like to try waterskiing	Quiero hacer ski aquático	Kee-e-ro a-thair es-kee a-kwa-tee-ko
I haven't tried it before	No lo he hecho antes	No lo e e-cho an-tes
Can I hire a wetsuit?	¿Puedo alquilar un traje de bucear?	Pwe-do al-kee-lar oon tra-he de boo-the-ar
Should I wear a life jacket?	¿Tengo que llevar salvavidas?	Ten-go ke llye-bar sal-ba-bee-das
Can I hire a rowing boat?	¿Puedo alquilar una barca de remar?	Pwe-do al-kee-lar oo-na bar-ka de re-mar
a motor boat?	lancha a motor?	lan-cha a mo-tor
a wind surfer?	tabla de surf?	ta-bla de soorf
Is there a map of the river?	¿Tiene un mapa del río?	Tee-e-ne oon ma-pa del **ree-o**
Are there many locks to pass?	¿Hay muchas esclusas?	Eye moo-chas es-kloo-sas
Can we get fuel here?	¿Podemos repostar combustible aquí?	Po-de-mos re-pos-tar kom-boos-tee-ble a-**kee**

THE BULLFIGHT[1]

the bull	el toro	to-ro
the bullfight	la corrida de toros	kor-ree-da de to-ros
the bullring	la plaza de toros	pla-tha de to-ros

1. La novillada is a corrida with young bulls and inexperienced bullfighters (novilleros).

tickets	entradas	en-tra-das
in the sun (*cheaper*)	... de sol	de sol
in the shade (*more expensive*)	... de sombra	de som-bra
ringside (*best*) seats	barreras	bar-rair-as
second-best seats	contrabarreras	kon-tra-bar-rair-ras
seats directly behind the **contrabarreras**	tendidos	ten-dee-dos
a box	un palco	pal-ko
the gods	la galería	ga-le-**ree**-a
the balcony	el balconcillo	bal-kon-thee-llyo
the bullfighter	el torero	to-re-ro
horsemen with lances who weaken the bull	los picadores	pee-ka-do-res
the men who place the darts in the bull's shoulder muscles	los banderilleros	ban-dair-ee-llye-ros
the darts	las banderillas	ban-dair-ee-llyas
red and yellow cloak used at the beginning of the **corrida**	la capa/el capote	ka-pa/ka-po-te
small cape used for dangerous passes and preparation for the kill	la muleta	moo-le-ta
the kill	la estocada	es-to-ka-da

the stabbing at the base of the skull if the bull is not killed immediately	**el descabello**	des-ka-be-llyo
the ear (the bullfighter may be awarded one or both ears or the tail, depending on his performance)	**la oreja**	o-re-ha
the tail	**el rabo**	ra-bo

ON THE BEACH[1]

Which is the best beach?	¿Cuál es la mejor playa?	Kwal es la me-hor pla-ya
Is there a quiet beach near here?	¿Hay por aquí alguna playa tranquila?	Eye por a-kee al-goo-na pla-ya tran-kee-la
Is it far to walk?	¿Se puede ir andando?	Se pwe-de eer an-dan-do
Is there a bus to the beach?	¿Hay autobús a la playa?	Eye ow-toh-**boos** a la pla-ya
Is the beach sand? pebbles? rocks?	¿Es la playa de arena? piedras? rocas?	Es la pla-ya de a-re-na pee-e-dras ro-kas
Is it safe for swimming?	¿Es seguro para nadar aquí?	Es se-goo-ro pa-ra na-dar a-kee
Is there a lifeguard?	¿Hay guarda/ salvavidas?	Eye gwar-da/sal-ba-bee-das

1. See also SPORTS & GAMES, (p. 156).

Is it safe for small children?	¿No es peligrosa para niños pequeños?	No es pe-lee-gro-sa pa-ra nee-nyos pe-ke-nyos
Does it get very rough?	¿Se pone el mar bravo?	Se po-ne el mar bra-bo
Bathing prohibited	*Prohibido bañarse	Pro-ee-bee-do ba-nyar-se
It's dangerous	*Hay peligro	Eye pel-ee-gro
What time is high/low tide?	¿A qué hora es la marea alta/baja?	A ke o-ra es la ma-re-a al-ta/ba-ha
Is the tide rising/ falling?	¿Está la marea subiendo/bajando?	Es-ta la ma-re-a soo-bee-en-do/ba-han-do
There's a strong current here	*Aquí hay mucha corriente	A-kee eye moo-cha kor-ree-en-te
You will be out of your depth	*No se hace pie	No se a-the pee-e
Are you a strong swimmer?	*¿Nada bien?	Na-da bee-en
Is it deep?	¿Hay mucha profundidad?	Eye moo-cha pro-foon-dee-dad
Is the water cold?	¿Está el agua fría?	Es-ta el a-gwa free-a
It's warm	Está caliente	Es-ta ka-lee-en-te
Can one swim in the lake/river?	¿Se puede nadar en el lago/río?	Se pwe-de na-dar en el la-go/ree-o
Is there an indoor/ outdoor swimming pool?	¿Hay piscina cubierta/al aire libre?	Eye pees-thee-na koo-bee-air-ta/al a-ee-re lee-bre
Is it salt or fresh water	¿Es agua dulce o salada?	Es a-gwa dul-the o sa-la-da
Are there showers?	¿Hay duchas?	Eye doo-chas

I want to hire a cabin	**Quiero alquilar una caseta**	Kee-e-ro al-kee-lar oon-a ka-se-ta
for the day	**para todo el día**	pa-ra to-do el **dee**-a
morning	**para la mañana**	pa-ra la ma-nya-na
two hours	**por dos horas**	por dos o-ras
I want to hire a deck chair/sunshade	**Quiero alquilar una hamaca/una sombrilla**	Kee-e-ro al-kee-lar oon-a a-ma-ka/oon-a som-bree-llya
Where can I buy	**¿Dónde puedo comprar**	Don-de pwe-do kom-prar
a snorkel?	**un tubo para bucear?**	oon too-bo pa-ra boo-the-ar
flippers?	**unas aletas?**	oon-as a-le-tas
a bucket and spade?	**un cubo y una paleta?**	oon koo-bo ee oo-na pa-le-ta
Where's the harbour?	**¿Dónde está el puerto?**	Don-de es-ta el pwair-to
Can we go out in a fishing boat?	**¿Se puede salir a pescar en barco?**	Se pwe-de sa-leer a pes-kar en bar-ko
Can I hire a rowing boat/motor boat?	**¿Se puede alquilar un barco de remar/una motora?**	Se pwe-de al-kee-lar oon bar-ko de re-mar/oon-a mo-to-ra
What does it cost by the hour?	**¿Cuánto cuesta por hora?**	Kwan-to kwes-ta por-or-a
beach bag	**el bolso playero**	bol-so pla-ye-ro
ball	**la pelota de playa**	pe-lo-ta de pla-ya
crab	**el cangrejo**	kan-gre-ho
first aid	**los primeros auxilios**	pree-me-ros a-oo-see-lyos
jelly fish	**la medusa**	me-doo-sa
lifebelt	**el salvavidas**	sal-ba-bee-das

lighthouse	**el faro**	fa-ro
rock	**la roca**	ro-ka
sand	**la arena**	a-re-na
sandbank	**el banco de arena**	ban-ko de a-re-na
sandcastle	**el castillo de arena**	kas-tee-llyo de a-re-na
sunglasses	**las gafas de sol**	ga-fas de sol
swimsuit	**el traje de baño**	tra-he de ban-yo
swimming trunks	**el bañador**	ba-nya-dor
towel	**la toalla**	to-a-llya
water-wings	**las aletas de agua**	a-le-tas de a-gwa
wave	**la ola**	o-la

IN THE COUNTRY[1]

Is there a scenic route to …?	¿Hay una ruta panorámica a …?	Eye oon-a roo-ta pa-no-ra-mee-ka a
Can you give me a lift to …?	¿Me puede llevar a …?	Me pwe-de llye-bar-a
Is there a footpath to …?	¿Hay una senda a …?	Eye oon-a sen-da a
Is it possible to go across country?	¿Se puede ir a campo través?	Se pwe-de eer a kam-po tra-bes
Is there a shortcut?	¿Hay algún atajo?	Eye al-goon a-ta-ho
Is this a public footpath?	¿Hay una senda pública?	Eye oon-a sen-da poo-blee-ka
Is there a bridge across the stream?	¿Hay un puente para cruzar el riachuelo?	Eye oon pwen-te pa-ra kroo-thar el ree-a-choo-e-lo
Can we walk?	¿Podemos ir andando?	Po-de-mos eer an-dan-do

1. See also DIRECTIONS (p. 33).

How far is the next village?	¿A cuánto está el próximo pueblo?	A kwan-to es-ta el pro-see-mo pwe-blo
How long is the walk to ...?	¿Qué distancia hay a ...?	Ke dees-tan-thee-a eye a
It's an hour's walk to ...	*Hay una hora de camino a ...	Eye oon-a o-ra de ka-mee-no a

THE WEATHER

Is it usually as hot as this?	¿Hace tanto calor normalmente?	A-the tan-to ka-lor nor-mal-men-te
It's going to be hot/cold today	*Hoy va a hacer calor/frío	Oy ba a a-thair ka-lor/free-o
The mist will clear later	*Luego se levanta la niebla	Lwe-go se le-ban-ta la nee-e-bla
Will it be fine tomorrow?	¿Hará buen tiempo mañana?	A-ra bwen tee-em-po ma-nya-na
Do you think it's going to rain/snow?	¿Cree que va a llover/nevar?	Kre-e ke ba a llyo-ber/ne-bar
What is the weather forecast?	¿Cuál es el parte metereológico?	Kwal es el par-te me-tair-re-o-lo-hee-ko

TRAVELLING WITH CHILDREN

Can you put a child's bed/cot in our room?	¿Puede poner una camita/cuna en nuestra habitación?	Pwe-de po-nair oon-a ka-mee-ta/koo-na en noo-es-tra a-bee-ta-thyon
Can you give us an adjoining room?	¿Nos puede dar las habitaciones contiguas?	Nos pwe-de dar las a-bee-ta-thyo-nes kon-tee-gwas
Does the hotel have a babysitting service?	¿Tiene este hotel servicio de niñeras/canguros?	Tee-e-ne es-te o-tel sair-bee-thyo de nee-nye-ras/kan-goo-ros
Can you find me a babysitter?	¿Puede buscarme una niñera/canguro?	Pwe-de boos-kar-me oon-a nee-nye-ra/kan-goo-ro

We shall be out for a couple of hours	Estaremos fuera dos horas	Es-ta-re-mos foo-e-ra dos o-ras
We shall be back at ...	Volveremos a las ...	Bol-be-rai-mos a las
Is there a children's menu?	¿Hay menú de niños?	Eye me-**noo** de nee-nyos
Do you have half portions for children?	¿Tiene raciones pequeñas para niños?	Tee-e-ne ra-thee-o-nes pe-ke-nyas pa-ra nee-nyos
Have you got a high chair?	¿Tiene sillita de niños?	Tee-ene see-llyee-ta de nee-nyos
Where can I feed/change my baby?	¿Dónde puedo dar de comer al niño/cambiar el niño?	Don-de pwe-do dar de ko-mair al nee-nyo/kam-byar el nee-nyo
Can you heat this bottle for me?	¿Puede calentarme el biberón?	Pwe-de ka-lain-tar-me el bee-be-**ron**
I want some disposable nappies a feeding bottle some baby food	Quiero pañales desechables un biberón potitos de niño	Kee-e-ro pa-nya-les de-se-cha-bles oon bee-be-**ron** po-tee-tos de nee-nyo
Are there any organized activities for children?	¿Organizan juegos para los niños?	Or-ga-nee-than hoo-e-gos pa-ra los nee-nyos

Is there a paddling pool/children's swimming pool?	¿Tienen piscina pequeña/piscina de niños?	Tee-e-nen pees-thee-na pe-ke-nya/pees-thee-na de nee-nyos
Is there a playground?	¿Hay algún parque infantil?	Eye al-goon par-ke een-fan-teel
a games room?	una sala de recreativos?	oo-na sa-la de re-kre-a-tee-bos
an amusement park?	una feria?	oo-na fe-ree-a
a zoo?	un parque zoológico?	oon par-ke tho-lo-hee-ko
a toyshop?	una tienda de juguetes?	oo-na tee-en-da de hoo-ge-tes
I'd like	Quiero	Kee-e-ro
a beach ball	una pelota para la playa	oon-a pe-lo-ta pa-ra la pla-ya
a bucket and spade	un cubo y una paleta	oon koo-bo ee oon-a pa-le-ta
a doll	una muñeca	oon-a moo-nye-ka
some flippers	unas aletas	oon-as a-le-tas
some goggles	unas gafas de bucear	oon-as ga-fas de boo-the-ar
some playing cards	una baraja	oon-a ba-ra-ha
some roller skates	unos patines	oon-os pa-tee-nes
a snorkel	un tubo de respirar bajo el agua	oon too-bo de res-pee-rar ba-ho el a-gwa

My daughter suffers from travel sickness	**Mi hija se marea en los viajes**	Mee ee-ha se ma-re-a en los bee-a-hes
She has hurt herself	**Ella se ha hecho daño**	E-llya se a e-cho da-nyo
My son is ill	**Mi hijo está enfermo**	Mee ee-ho es-ta en-fair-mo
He has lost his toy	**El ha perdido su juguete**	El a pair-dee-do soo hoo-ge-te
I'm sorry if they have bothered you	**Siento si lo han molestado**	See-en-to see lo an mo-les-ta-do

BUSINESS MATTERS[1]

I would like to make an appointment with ...	Quiero concertar una hora con ...	Kee-e-ro kon-thair-tar oon-a o-ra kon ...
I have an appointment with ...	Tengo una cita con ...	Ten-go oon-a thee-ta kon ...
My name is ...	Me llamo ...	Me llya-mo
Here is my card	Aquí tiene mi tarjeta	A-kee tee-e-ne mee tar-he-ta
This is our catalogue	Este es nuestro catálogo	Es-te es nwes-tro ka-ta-lo-go
I would like to see your products	Quiero ver sus productos	Kee-e-ro bair soos pro-dook-tos

1. See also TELEPHONING (p. 143).

Could you send me some examples?	¿Me puede mandar muestras?	Me pwe-de man-dar moo-es-tras
Can you provide an interpreter/a secretary?	¿Puede traer un intérprete/una secretaria?	Pwe-de tra-er oon een-tair-pre-te/oon-a se-kre-ta-ree-a
Where can I make some photocopies?	¿Dónde puedo sacar fotocopias?	Don-de pwe-do sa-kar fo-to-ko-pee-as

AT THE DOCTOR'S

Is there a doctor's surgery nearby?	¿Hay algún dispensario cerca?	Eye al-**goon** dees-pen-sa-ree-o thair-ka
I must see a doctor. Can you recommend one?	Quiero que me vea un médico. ¿Puede recomendarme alguno?	Kee-e-ro ke me bea oon me-dee-ko. Pwe-de re-ko-men-dar-me al-goo-no
Please call a doctor	Llame al médico, por favor	Llya-me al me-dee-ko por fa-bor
When can the doctor come?	¿Cuándo puede venir el médico?	Kwan-do pwe-de be-neer el me-dee-ko
Does the doctor speak English?	¿Habla el médico inglés?	Ab-la el me-dee-ko een-gles
Can I make an appointment for as soon as possible?	¿Puedo tener hora lo antes posible?	Pwe-do te-nair o-ra lo an-tes po-see-ble

AILMENTS

I am ill	No me encuentro bien	No me en-koo-en-tro bee-en
I take ..., can you give me a prescription please?	Estoy tomando ..., ¿me puede dar una receta?	Es-toy to-man-do ... me pwe-de dar oon-a re-the-ta
I am allergic to ...	Soy alérgico a ...	Soy a-**ler**-hee-ko a
I have a fever	Tengo temperatura	Ten-go tem-pair-a-too-ra
I have a cardiac condition	Sufro del corazón	Soo-fro del ko-ra-**thon**
I have high/low blood pressure	Tengo la tensión alta/baja	Ten-go la ten-**syon** al-ta/ba-ha
I am pregnant	Estoy en estado	Es-toy en es-ta-do
I think it is infected	Creo que está infectado	Kre-o ke es-**ta** een-fek-ta-do
I've a pain in my right/left arm	Me duele el brazo derecho/izquierdo	Me doo-e-le el bra-tho de-re-cho/eeth-kyair-do
My wrist hurts	Me duele la muñeca	Me doo-e-le la moo-nye-ka
I think I've sprained/broken my ankle	Creo que me he dislocado/roto el tobillo	Kre-o ke me e dees-lo-ka-do/ro-to el to-bee-llyo
I fell down and my back hurts	Me he caído y me duele la espalda	Me e ka-**ee**-do ee me doo-e-le la es-pal-da

My foot is swollen	**Tengo el pie hinchado**	Ten-go el pee-e een-cha-do
I've burned/cut/ bruised myself	**Me he quemado/ cortado/dado un golpe**	Me e ke-ma-do/kor-ta-do/da-do oon gol-pe
My stomach is upset	**Tengo mal el estómago**	Ten-go mal el es-to-ma-go
I have indigestion	**No hago bien la digestión/tengo indigestión**	No a-go bee-en la dee-hes-tyon/ten-go een-dee-hes-tyon
My appetite's gone	**No tengo apetito**	No ten-go ape-tee-to
I think I've got food poisoning	**Creo que estoy intoxicado**	Kre-o ke es-toy een-to-see-ka-do
I can't eat/sleep	**No puedo comer/ dormir**	No pwe-do ko-mer/dor-meer
I am a diabetic	**Soy diabético**	Soy dee-a-be-tee-ko
My nose keeps bleeding	**Sangro por la nariz frecuentemente**	San-gro por la nar-eeth fre-koo-en-te-men-te
I have earache	**Me duelen los oídos**	Me doo-e-len los o-ee-dos
I have difficulty in breathing	**No respiro bien**	No res-pee-ro bee-en
I feel dizzy	**Me siento mareado**	Me see-en-to ma-re-a-do
I feel shivery	**Tengo escalofríos**	Ten-go es-ka-lo-free-os
I feel sick	**Tengo náuseas/ganas de devolver**	Ten-go naw-se-as/ga-nas de de-bol-bair
I keep vomiting	**Tengo vómitos**	Ten-go bo-mee-tos
I think I've caught flu	**Creo que tengo gripe**	Kre-o ke ten-go gree-pe
I've got a cold	**Tengo catarro**	Ten-go ka-tar-ro

I've had it since yesterday/for a few hours	**Lo tengo desde ayer/desde hace unas horas**	Lo ten-go des-de a-yair/ des-de a-the oon-as o-ras
abscess	**el absceso**	ab-the-so
ache	**el dolor**	do-lor
allergy	**la alergia**	al-air-hee-a
appendicitis	**la apendicitis**	apen-dee-thee-tees
asthma	**el asma**	as-ma
back pain	**el dolor de espalda**	do-lor de es-pal-da
blister	**la ampolla**	am-poll-ya
boil	**el forúnculo**	for-**oon**-koo-lo
bruise	**la moradura**	mo-ra-doo-ra
burn	**la quemadura**	ke-ma-doo-ra
chill	**el enfriamiento**	en-free-a-myen-to
constipation	**el estreñimiento**	es-tren-yee-myen-to
cough	**la tos**	toss
cramp	**el calambre**	ka-lam-bray
diabetic	**diabético**	dya-**be**-tee-ko
diarrhoea	**la diarrea**	dee-or-ray-a
earache	**el dolor de oídos**	do-lor de o-**ee**-dos
fever	**la fiebre**	fye-bre
food poisoning	**la intoxicación**	een-tok-see-ka-**thyon**
fracture	**la fractura**	frak-too-ra
hay fever	**la alergia al polen**	al-air-hee-a al po-len
headache	**el dolor de cabeza**	do-lor de ka-be-tha
heart condition	**sufro del corazón**	soo-fro del ko-ra-**thon**
high blood pressure	**la tensión alta**	ten-**syon** al-ta

ill, sick	**enfermo**	en-fair-mo
illness	**la enfermedad**	en-fair-me-dad
indigestion	**la indigestión**	een-dee-hes-**tyon**
infection	**la infección**	een-fek-**thyon**
influenza	**la gripe**	gree-pe
insect bite	**la picadura de insecto**	pee-ka-doo-ra de een-sek-to
insomnia	**el insomnio**	een-som-nyo
nausea	**la naúsea**	now-se-a
nose bleed	**la hemorragia nasal**	e-mo-rra-hee-a na-sal
pain	**el dolor**	do-lor
rheumatism	**el reumatismo**	ray-oom-at-ees-mo
sore throat	**la garganta irritada**	gar-gan-ta ee-ree-ta-da
sting	**la picadura**	pee-ka-doo-ra
stomach ache	**el dolor de estómago**	do-lor de es-to-ma-go
sunburn	**la quemadura de sol**	ke-mah-doo-ra de sol
sunstroke	**la insolación**	een-so-la-**thyon**
swelling	**el hinchazón**	een-cha-**thon**
toothache	**el dolor de muelas**	do-lor de mwe-las
ulcer	**la úlcera**	ool-ther-a
wound	**la herida**	ay-ree-da

TREATMENT

| Do you have a temperature? | *¿Tiene algo de temperatura? | Tee-e-ne al-go de tem-pe-ra-too-ra |

Where does it hurt?	*¿Dónde le duele?	Don-de le dwe-le
Have you a pain here?	*¿Le duele aquí?	Le dwe-le a-kee
How long have you had the pain?	*¿Desde cuánto le duele?	Des-de kwan-to le dwe-le
Open your mouth	*Abra la boca	Ab-ra la bo-ka
Put out your tongue	*Saque la lengua	Sa-ke la len-gwa
Breathe in	*Respire fuerte	Res-pee-re fwer-te
Breathe out	*Espire	Es-pee-re
Does that hurt?	*¿Le duele ahí?	Le dwe-le a-ee
A lot?	*¿Mucho?	Moo-cho
A little?	*¿Un poco?	Oon po-ko
Please lie down	*Acuéstese	A-kwes-te-se
I will need a specimen	*Necesito una muestra	Ne-the-see-to oon-a moo-es-tra
What medicines have you been taking?	*¿Qué medicinas ha estado tomando?	Ke me-dee-thee-nas a es-ta-do to-man-do
I take this medicine; could you give me another prescription?	Tomo estas medicinas; ¿podría recetármelas?	To-mo es-tas me-dee-thee-nas po-dree-a re-the-tar-me-las
I'll give you some pills/medicine	*Voy a darle unas píldoras/una medicina	Boy a dar-le oon-as peel-do-ras/oon-a me-dee-thee-na
I will give you an antibiotic	*Le voy a dar un antibiótico	Le boy a dar oon an-tee-bee-o-tee-ko
a painkiller	un calmante	oon kal-man-te
a sedative	un sedante	oon se-dan-te

Are you allergic to antibiotics?	*¿Es usted alérgico a los antibióticos?	Es oos-ted a-**lair**-hee-ko a los an-tee-bee-**o**-tee-kos
Take this prescription to the chemist's	*Lleve esta receta a la farmacia	Llye-be es-ta re-the-ta a la far-**ma**-thee-a
Take this three times a day	*Tome la medicina tres veces al día	To-me la me-dee-thee-na tres be-thes al **dee**-a
I'll give you an injection	*Voy a ponerle una inyección	Boy a po-nair-le oon-a een-yek-**thyon**
Roll up your sleeve	*Súbase la manga	Soo-ba-se la man-ga
I'll put you on a diet	*Voy a ponerle un régimen	Boy a po-nair-le oon re-**hee**-men
Come and see me again in two days	*Vuelva dentro de dos días	Bwel-ba den-tro de dos **dee**-as
You must be X-rayed	*Tiene que hacerse una radiografía	Tee-e-ne ke a-**thair**-se oon-a ra-dee-o-gra-**fee**-a
You must go to hospital	*Tiene usted que ir a un hospital/una clínica	Tee-e-ne oos-te ke eer a oon os-pee-tal/oon-a **klee**-nee-ka
You're hurting me	Me hace daño	Me a-the da-nyo
Must I stay in bed?	¿Tengo que estar en la cama?	Ten-go ke es-tar en la ka-ma
Will you call again?	¿Volverá usted?	Bol-bair-**a** oos-te
When can I travel again?	¿Cuándo podré viajar?	Kwan-do po-**dre** bee-a-har
You should not travel until ...	*No debiera viajar hasta ...	No de-bye-ra bee-a-har as-ta
Nothing to worry about	*No tiene nada para preocuparse	No tee-e-ne na-da pa-ra pre-o-koo-par-se

I feel better now	**Estoy mejor**	Es-toy me-hor
How much do I owe you?	**¿Cuánto le debo?**	Kwan-to le de-bo
I'd like a receipt for the health insurance	**Quiero un recibo para el seguro de enfermedad**	Kee-e-ro oon re-thee-bo pa-ra el se-goo-ro de en-fer-me-dad
ambulance	**la ambulancia**	am-boo-lan-thya
anaesthetic	**el anestésico**	anes-tes-ee-ko
aspirin	**la aspirina**	as-pee-ree-na
bandage	**la venda**	ben-da
chiropodist	**el pedicuro**	pe-dee-koo-ro
hospital	**el hospital**	os-pee-tal
injection	**la inyección**	een-yek-**thyon**
laxative	**el laxante**	lak-san-te
nurse	**la enfermera**	en-fair-mair-a
operation	**la operación**	o-pair-a-**thyon**
optician	**el óptico**	op-tee-ko
pill	**la píldora**	**peel**-do-ra
(adhesive) plaster	**el esparadrapo/tiritas**	es-pa-ra-dra-po/tee-ree-tas
prescription	**la receta**	re-the-ta
X-ray	**la radiografía**	ra-dyo-gra-**fee**-a

PARTS OF THE BODY

| ankle | **el tobillo** | to-bee-llyo |
| arm | **el brazo** | bra-tho |

back	**la espalda**	es-pal-da
bladder	**la vesícula**	bes-ee-koo-la
blood	**la sangre**	san-gre
body	**el cuerpo**	kwair-po
bone	**el hueso**	oo-e-**so**
brain	**el seso/el cerebro**	se-so/the-re-bro
breast	**el pecho**	pe-cho
cheek	**la mejilla**	me-hee-llya
chest	**el pecho**	pe-cho
chin	**la barbilla**	bar-bee-llya
ear	**la oreja**	or-ay-ha
elbow	**el codo**	ko-do
eye	**el ojo**	o-ho
face	**la cara**	ka-ra
finger	**el dedo**	de-do
foot	**el pie**	pee-ay
forehead	**la frente**	fren-te
gums	**la encía**	en-**thee**-a
hand	**la mano**	ma-no
head	**la cabeza**	kab-ay-tha
heart	**el corazón**	ko-ra-**thon**
heel	**el talón**	ta-**lon**
hip	**la cadera**	ka-dair-a
jaw	**la mandíbula**	man-**dee**-boo-la
kidney	**el riñón**	reen-yon
knee	**la rodilla**	ro-dee-llya

knee cap	**la rótula**	ro-too-la
leg	**la pierna**	pee-air-na
lip	**el labio**	la-bee-o
liver	**el hígado**	ee-ga-do
lung	**el pulmón**	pool-mon
mouth	**la boca**	bo-ka
muscle	**el músculo**	moos-koo-lo
nail	**la uña**	oon-ya
neck	**el cuello**	kwe-llyo
nerve	**el nervio**	nair-byo
nose	**la nariz**	na-reeth
rib	**la costilla**	kos-tee-llya
shoulder	**la espalda**	es-pal-da
skin	**la piel**	pee-el
spine	**la espina dorsal**	es-pee-na dor-sal
stomach	**el estómago**	es-to-ma-go
thigh	**el muslo**	moos-lo
throat	**la garganta**	gar-gan-ta
thumb	**el pulgar**	pool-gar
toe	**el dedo del pie**	de-do del pee-ay
tongue	**la lengua**	len-gwa
tonsils	**las amígdalas**	a-meeg-da-las
tooth	**el diente**	dyen-te
vein	**la vena**	be-na
wrist	**la muñeca**	moon-ye-ka

AT THE DENTIST'S

I must see a dentist	**Quiero ir al dentista**	Kee-e-ro eer al den-tees-ta
Can I make an appointment?	**¿Pueden darme hora?**	Pwe-den dar-me o-ra
As soon as possible	**Lo antes posible**	Lo an-tes po-see-ble
I have toothache	**Me duelen las muelas**	Ma dwe-len las mwe-las
This tooth hurts	**Me duele este diente**	Me dwe-le es-te dyen-te
I have a broken tooth	**Se me ha roto un diente/una muela**	Se me a ro-to oon dyen-te/oon-a mwe-la
I've lost a filling	**Se me ha caído un empaste**	Se me a ka-ee-do oon em-pas-te
Can you fill it?	**¿Puede empastarme un diente?**	Pwe-de em-pas-tar-me oon dyen-te
Can you do it now?	**¿Puede hacérmelo ahora?**	Pwe-de a-**thair**-me-lo a-ora
Will you take the tooth out?	**¿Tiene que sacarme la muela?**	Tee-e-ne ke sa-kar-me la mwe-la

I do not want the tooth taken out	**No quiero sacarme el diente**	No kee-e-ro sa-kar-me el dyen-te
Please give me an anaesthetic	**Por favor déme anestético**	Por fa-bor **de**-me oon a-nes-**te**-tee-ko
My gums are swollen/keep bleeding	**Tengo las encías inflamadas/me sangran las encías**	Ten-go las en-**thee**-as een-fla-ma-das/me san-gran las en-**thee**-as
I have broken my dentures	**Se me ha roto la dentadura**	Se me a ro-to la den-ta-doo-ra
Can you fix it (temporarily)?	**¿Puede arreglármelo (temporalmente)?**	Pwe-de ar-reg-**lar**-me-lo (tem-po-ral-men-te)
You're hurting me	**Me está haciendo mucho daño**	Me es-**ta** a-thee-en-do moo-cho da-nyo
How much do I owe you?	**¿Cuánto es, por favor?**	Kwan-to es por fa-bor
When should I come again?	**¿Cuándo tengo que volver?**	Kwan-do ten-go ke bol-bair
Please rinse your mouth	***Enjuágese**	En-hwa-ge-se
I will X-ray your teeth	***Tengo que hacerle una radiografía**	Ten-go ke a-thair-le oon-a ra-dee-o-gra-fee-a
You have an abscess	***Tiene usted un absceso**	Tee-e-ne oos-te oon oon ab-the-so
The nerve is exposed	***El nervio está al descubierto**	El nair-bee-o es-**ta** al des-koo-bee-air-to
This tooth can't be saved	***Esta muela no se puede salvar**	Es-ta mwe-la no se pwe-de sal-bar

PROBLEMS & ACCIDENTS

Where's the police station?	¿Dónde está la comisaría?	Don-de es-ta la ko-mee-sa-ree-a
Call the police	Llame a la policía	Llya-me a la po-lee-thee-a
Where is the British consulate?	¿Dónde está el consulado inglés?	Don-de es-ta el kon-soo-la-do een-gles
Please let the consulate know	Comuniquen con el consulado	Ko-moo-nee-ken kon el kon-soo-la-do
It's urgent	Es urgente	Es oor-hen-te
There's a fire	Hay fuego	Ay foo-e-go
My son/daughter is lost	Se ha perdido mi hijo/hija	Se a pair-dee-do mee ee-ho ee-ha
Our car has been broken into	Han robado un coche	An ro-ba-do oon ko-che
I've been robbed/ mugged	Me han robado	Me an ro-ba-do
My bag has been stolen	Me han robado el bolso	Me an ro-ba-do el bol-so

I found this in the street	**He encontrado esto en la calle**	E en-kon-tra-do es-to en la ka-llye
I have lost my luggage my passport my travellers' cheques	**He perdido mi equipaje mi pasaporte mis cheques de viajero**	E pair-dee-do mee e-kee-pa-he mee pa-sa-por-te mees che-kes de bya-hai-ro
I have missed my train	**He perdido el tren**	E pair-dee-do el tren
My luggage is on board	**Mi equipaje está en el tren**	Mee e-kee-pa-he es-ta en el tren
Call a doctor	**Llame a un médico**	Llya-me a oon me-dee-ko
Call an ambulance	**Llame una ambulancia**	Llya-me oon-a am-boo-lan-thya
There has been an accident	**Ha habido un accidente**	A ab-ee-do oon ak-thee-den-te
We've had an accident	**Hemos tenido un accidente**	E-mos te-nee-do oon ak-thee-den-te
He's badly hurt	**Está gravemente herido**	Es-ta gra-be-mente e-ree-do
He has fainted	**Se ha desmayado**	Se a des-ma-ya-do
He's losing blood	**Está perdiendo sangre**	Es-ta pair-dee-en-do san-gre
Her arm is broken	**Su brazo esta roto**	Soo bra-tho es-ta ro-to
Please get some water/a blanket/ some bandages	**(Traiga) agua/una manta/vendas, por favor**	(Tra-ee-ga) a-gwa/oon-a man-ta/ben-das por fa-bor
I've broken my glasses	**Se me han roto las gafas**	Se me an ro-to las ga-fas
I can't see	**No puedo ver**	No pwe-do bair

A child has fallen in the water	**Se ha caído al agua un niño**	Se a ka-ee-do al a-gwa oon nee-nyo
A woman is drowning	**Se está ahogando una mujer**	Se es-ta a-o-gan-do oon-a moo-hair
May I see your insurance certificate/driving licence	***Quiero ver su póliza de seguros/carnet de conducir**	Kee-e-ro bair soo po-lee-tha de se-goo-ros/kar-net de kon-doo-theer
I didn't understand the sign	**No entendía la señal**	No en-ten-dee-a la se-nyal
How much is the fine?	**¿Cuánto es la multa?**	Kwan-to es la mool-ta
Apply to the insurance company	***Diríjase a la compañía de seguros**	Dee-ree-ha-se a la kom-pa-nya de se-goo-ros
Can you help me?	**¿Puede ayudarme?**	Pwe-de a-yoo-dar-me
What is the name and address of the owner?	**¿Cuál es el nombre y dirección del propietario?**	Kwal es el nom-bre ee dee-rek-thyon del pro-pye-ta-ryo
Are you willing to act as a witness?	**¿Está usted dispuesto a servir de testigo?**	Es-ta oost-e dees-poo-es-to a ser-beer de tes-tee-go
Can I have your name and address please?	**Su nombre y dirección, por favor**	Soo nom-bre ee dee-rek-thyon por fa-bor

TIME & DATES

TIME

What time is it?	**¿Qué hora es?**	Ke o-ra es
It's one o'clock	**Es la una**	Es la oon-a
It's two o'clock	**Son las dos**	Son las dos
quarter to ten	**las diez menos cuarto**	dy-eth me-nos kwar-to
quarter past five	**las cinco y cuarto**	theen-ko ee kwar-to
half past four	**las cuatro y media**	kwa-tro ee me-dee-a
five past eight	**las ocho y cinco**	o-cho ee theen-ko
twenty to three	**las tres menos veinte**	tres me-nos beyn-te
twenty-five to seven	**las siete menos veinticinco**	sye-te me-nos beyn-tee-theen-ko
twenty-five past eight	**las ocho y veinticinco**	o-cho ee beyn-tee-theen-ko

second	el segundo	se-goon-do
minute	el minuto	mee-noo-to
hour	la hora	o-ra
It's early/late	Es temprano/tarde	Es tem-pra-no/tar-de
My watch is slow/fast	Mi reloj está astrasado/ adelantado	Mee re-loh es-ta atra-sa-do/ade-lan-ta-do
The clock has stopped	Se ha parado el reloj	Se a pa-ra-do el re-loh
Sorry I am late	Perdone mi retraso	Pair-do-n-e mee re-tra-so

DATE

What's the date?	¿A cuántos estamos?/¿qué día es hoy?	A kwan-tos es-ta-mos/ke dee-a es oy
It's 9th December[1]	Hoy es el nueve de diciembre	Oy es el nwe-be de dee-thyem-bre
We're leaving on 5th January	Nos marchamos el cinco de enero	Nos mar-cha-mos el theen-ko de e-nair-o
We got here on 27th July	Llegamos el veintisiete de julio	Llye-ga-mos el beyn-tee-sye-te de hoo-lyo

DAY

morning	la mañana	ma-nya-na
this morning	esta mañana	es-ta ma-nya-na
in the morning	por la mañana	por la ma-nya-na

1. Cardinal numbers are used for dates in Spanish, except for 1st which is **primero**.

midday, noon	**mediodía**	me-dee-o-**dee**-a
afternoon	**la tarde**	tar-de
yesterday afternoon	**ayer por la tarde**	a-yair por la tar-de
dusk, nightfall[1]	**el anochecer**	a-no-che-thair
midnight	**medianoche**	me-dee-a-no-che
night	**la noche**	no-che
tonight	**esta noche**	es-ta no-che
tomorrow night	**mañana por la noche**	ma-nya-na por la no-che
sunrise	**el amanecer**	a-ma-ne-thair
dawn	**la madrugada**	ma-droo-ga-da
sunset, twilight	**el crepúsculo**	cre-**poo**-scoo-lo
today	**hoy**	oy
yesterday	**ayer**	a-yair
day before yesterday	**anteayer**	an-te-a-yair
tomorrow	**mañana**	ma-nya-na
day after tomorrow	**pasado mañana**	pa-sa-do ma-nya-na
in ten days' time	**dentro de diez días**	den-tro de dyeth **dee**-as

WEEK

Sunday	**domingo**	do-meen-go
Monday	**lunes**	loo-nes
Tuesday	**martes**	mar-tes

1. Spanish has no exact equivalent of the English word 'evening': **la tarde** is used if the time is before sunset; **la noche** if it is after.

Wednesday	**miércoles**	myair-ko-les
Thursday	**jueves**	hwe-bes
Friday	**viernes**	byair-nes
Saturday	**sábado**	sa-ba-do
on Tuesday	**el martes**	mar-tes
on Sundays	**los domingos**	do-meen-gos
fortnight	**quince días/dos semanas**	keen-the **dee**-as dos se-ma-nas

MONTH

January	**enero**	e-nair-o
February	**febrero**	feb-rair-o
March	**marzo**	mar-tho
April	**abril**	ab-reel
May	**mayo**	ma-yo
June	**junio**	hoo-nyo
July	**julio**	hoo-lyo
August	**agosto**	agos-toh
September	**setiembre**	se-tyem-bre
October	**octubre**	ok-too-bre
November	**noviembre**	no-byem-bre
December	**diciembre**	dee-thyem-bre

SEASON

spring	**la primavera**	pree-ma-bair-a
summer	**el verano**	bair-ra-no
autumn	**el otoño**	oton-yo
winter	**el invierno**	een-byair-no
in spring	**en primavera**	en pree-ma-bair-a
during the summer	**durante el verano**	doo-ran-te el bai-ra-no

YEAR

this year	**este año**	es-te an-yo
last year	**el año pasado**	an-yo pa-sa-do
next year	**el próximo año/el año que viene**	pro-see-mo an-yo/el an-yo kay bye-ne

PUBLIC HOLIDAYS[1]

1 January	(New Year's Day)	**Año nuevo**
6 January	(Epiphany)	**Día de Reyes**
19 March	(St Joseph's Day)	**San José**
Good Friday		**Viernes santo**
Ascension Day		**Día de la Ascensión**
Corpus Christi		**Corpus Cristi**

1. Apart from these holidays every town and village celebrates its own holiday which usually coincides with the day of its patron saint.

25 July   (St James's Day)   **Día de Santiago (patron saint of Spain)**

15 August   (Assumption Day)   **Día de la Asunción**

12 October   (Columbus Day)   **Fiesta de la Hispanidad**

1 November   (All Saints' Day)   **Todos los Santos**

8 December   (Immaculate Conception Day)   **Inmaculada Concepción**

25 December   (Christmas)   **Navidad**

NUMBERS

CARDINAL

0	**cero**	the-ro
1	**uno/un, una**	oo-no/oon, oo-na
2	**dos**	dos
3	**tres**	tres
4	**cuatro**	kwa-tro
5	**cinco**	theen-ko
6	**seis**	says
7	**siete**	sye-te
8	**ocho**	ocho
9	**nueve**	nwe-be
10	**diez**	dyeth
11	**once**	on-the
12	**doce**	do-the

13	**trece**	tre-the
14	**catorce**	ka-tor-the
15	**quince**	keen-the
16	**diez y seis/dieciseis**	dyeth ee says
17	**diez y siete/diecisiete**	dyeth ee sye-te
18	**diez y ocho/ dieciocho**	dyeth ee ocho
19	**diez y nueve/ diecinueve**	dyeth ee nwe-be
20	**veinte**	beyn-te
21	**veintiuno**	ben-tee-oo-no
22	**veintidós**	ben-tee-**dos**
30	**treinta**	tre-een-ta
31	**treinta y uno**	tre-een-ta-ee-oo-no
40	**cuarenta**	kwa-ren-ta
41	**cuarenta y uno**	kwa-ren-ta-ee-oo-no
50	**cincuenta**	theen-kwen-ta
51	**cincuenta y uno**	theen-kwen-ta-ee-oo-no
60	**sesenta**	se-sen-ta
61	**sesenta y uno**	se-sen-ta-ee-oo-no
70	**setenta**	se-ten-ta
71	**setenta y uno**	se-ten-ta-ee-oo-no
80	**ochenta**	o-chen-ta
81	**ochenta y uno**	o-chen-ta-ee-oo-no
90	**noventa**	no-ben-ta
91	**noventa y uno**	no-ben-ta-ee-oo-no
100	**cien/ciento**	thyen/thyen-to

101	**ciento uno**	thyen-to oo-no
200	**doscientos**	dos-thyen-tos
500	**quinientos**	kin-yen-tos
700	**setecientos**	se-te-thyen-tos
1000	**mil**	meel
2000	**dos mil**	dos meel
1,000,000	**un millón**	mee-llyon

ORDINAL

1st	**primero/primer, primera**	pree-mair-o/pree-mair, pree-mair-a
2nd	**segundo, -a**	se-goon-do
3rd	**tercero, -a**	tair-thair-o
4th	**cuarto, -a**	kwar-to
5th	**quinto, -a**	keen-to
6th	**sexto, -a**	ses-to
7th	**séptimo, -a**	sep-tee-mo
8th	**octavo, -a**	ok-ta-bo
9th	**noveno, -a**	no-be-no
10th	**décimo, -a**	de-thee-mo
half	**medio, -a/la mitad**	me-dee-o/mee-ta
quarter	**un cuarto**	kwar-to
three quarters	**tres cuartos**	tres kwar-tos
a third	**un tercio**	tair-thyo
two thirds	**dos tercios**	dos tair-thyos

WEIGHTS & MEASURES

DISTANCE

kilometres – miles

km	miles or km	miles	km	miles or km	miles
1.6	1	0.6	14.5	9	5.6
3.2	2	1.2	16.1	10	6.2
4.8	3	1.9	32.2	20	12.4
6.4	4	2.5	40.2	25	15.3
8.0	5	3.1	80.5	50	31.1
9.7	6	3.7	160.9	100	62.1
11.3	7	4.3	804.7	500	310.7
12.9	8	5.0			

A rough way to convert from miles to km: divide by 5 and multiply by 8; from km to miles divide by 8 and multiply by 5.

LENGTH AND HEIGHT

centimetres – inches

cm	ins or cm	ins	cm	ins or cm	ins
2.5	1	0.4	17.8	7	2.8
5.1	2	0.8	20.3	8	3.2
7.6	3	1.2	22.9	9	3.5
10.2	4	1.6	25.4	10	3.9
12.7	5	2.0	50.8	20	7.9
15.2	6	2.4	127.0	50	19.7

A rough way to convert from inches to cm: divide by 2 and multiply by 5; from cm to inches divide by 5 and multiply by 2.

metres – feet

m	ft or m	ft	m	ft or m	ft
0.3	1	3.3	2.4	8	26.2
0.6	2	6.6	2.7	9	29.5
0.9	3	9.8	3.0	10	32.8
1.2	4	13.1	6.1	20	65.6
1.5	5	16.4	15.2	50	164.0
1.8	6	19.7	30.5	100	328.1
2.1	7	23.0			

A rough way to convert from ft to m: divide by 10 and multiply by 3; from m to ft divide by 3 and multiply by 10.

metres – yards

m	yds or m	yds	m	yds or m	yds
0.9	1	1.1	7.3	8	8.7
1.8	2	2.2	8.2	9	9.8
2.7	3	3.3	9.1	10	10.9
3.7	4	4.4	18.3	20	21.9
4.6	5	5.5	45.7	50	54.7
5.5	6	6.6	91.4	100	109.4
6.4	7	7.7	457.2	500	546.8

A rough way to convert from yds to m: subtract 10 per cent from the number of yds; from m to yds add 10 per cent to the number of metres.

LIQUID MEASURES

litres – gallons

litres	galls or litres	galls	litres	galls or litres	galls
4.6	1	0.2	36.4	8	1.8
9.1	2	0.4	40.9	9	2.0
13.6	3	0.7	45.5	10	2.2
18.2	4	0.9	90.9	20	4.4
22.7	5	1.1	136.4	30	6.6
27.3	6	1.3	181.8	40	8.8
31.8	7	1.5	227.3	50	11.0

A rough way to convert from galls to litres: divide by 2 and multiply by 9; from litres to galls, divide by 9 and multiply by 2.

WEIGHT

kilogrammes – pounds

kg	lb. or kg	lb.	kg	lb. or kg	lb.
0.5	1	2.2	3.2	7	15.4
0.9	2	4.4	3.6	8	17.6
1.4	3	6.6	4.1	9	19.8
1.8	4	8.8	4.5	10	22.0
2.3	5	11.0	9.1	20	44.1
2.7	6	13.2	22.7	50	110.2

A rough way to convert from lb. to kg: divide by 11 and multiply by 5; from kg to lb. divide by 5 and multiply by 11.

grammes – ounces

grammes	oz.	oz.	grammes
100	3.5	2	56.7
250	8.8	4	113.4
500	17.6	8	226.8
1000 (1 kg)	35.0	16 (1 lb.)	453.6

TEMPERATURE

centigrade (°C) – fahrenheit (°F)

°C	°F	°C	°F	°C	°F
− 10	14	15	59	37	98.4
− 5	23	20	68	38	100.5
0	32	25	77	39	102
5	41	30	86	40	104
10	50	35	95	100	212

To convert °F to °C: deduct 32, divide by 9, multiply by 5; to convert °C to °F; divide by 5, multiply by 9 and add 32.

BASIC GRAMMAR

NOUNS

Nouns in Spanish are either masculine or feminine.

Nouns denoting males are masculine, as are most nouns ending in **-o**.

Nouns denoting females are feminine, as are most nouns ending in **-a**.

   e.g. **tío** – uncle; **vaso** – glass; **tía** – aunt; **playa** – beach.

Plural

The plural is formed by adding **-s** if the word ends in a vowel;

-es if it ends in a consonant.

   e.g. peseta – peseta**s**; tren (train) – tren**es**.

DEFINITE ARTICLE – the

el before a masculine singular noun   **el banco** (the bank)
los before a masculine plural noun   **los bancos**
la before a feminine singular noun   **la peseta**
las before a feminine plural noun   **las pesetas**

INDEFINITE ARTICLE – a, an

un before a masculine singular noun   **un banco**
una before a feminine singular noun   **una peseta**

ADJECTIVES

Adjectives agree in number and gender with the noun.

Those ending in **-o** change to **-a** in the feminine.

e.g. fres**co** – fres**ca** (fresh, cool).

Those ending in **-e** and most of those ending in a consonant are the same in the masculine and the feminine.

e.g. el coche grande; la casa grande (the big car; the big house).

The plural is formed by adding **-s** if the word ends in a vowel, **-es** if it ends in a consonant.

e.g. fresco – frescos; azul (blue) – azules.

The comparative and superlative are formed by putting **más** before the adjective.

e.g. un hotel barato   a cheap hotel
     un hotel **más** barato   a cheaper hotel
     el hotel **más** barato de la ciudad   the cheapest hotel
                                        in the town

POSSESSIVE ADJECTIVES

	s	*pl*		*s*	*pl*
my	mi	mis	their, your (*polite*)	su	sus
your (*familiar*)	tu	tus	our	nuestro	nuestros
his, her	su	sus	your (*familiar*)	vuestro	vuestros

These adjectives agree with the thing possessed, e.g. mi casa (my house); mis casas (my houses); vuestro libro (your book); vuestra carta (your letter).

PERSONAL PRONOUNS

	subject	*object*
I	yo	me
you (*familiar*)	tú	te
you (*polite*)	usted	le (*m*), la (*f*)
he	él	le
she	ella	la
it	él/ella	lo
we	nosotros/-as	nos
you (*familiar*)	vosotros/-as	os
you (*polite*)	ustedes	los (*m*), las (*f*)
they *m*	ellos	los
they *f*	ellas	las

Personal pronouns are usually omitted before the verb.

e.g. voy – I go; viene – he (she) comes.

Direct object pronouns are usually placed before the verb.

e.g. **me** ve – he sees me.

Indirect object pronouns are the same as direct object pronouns except that **le** is used to mean to him, to her, to it, to you (*polite*), and **les** means to them and to you (*polite*). If a direct and an indirect object pronoun are used together, the indirect one is placed first.

e.g. me **lo** da – he gives it to me.

If both pronouns are in the third person, **se** is used as indirect object.

e.g. **se** lo da – he gives it to him.

When speaking to strangers always use the forms **usted** and **ustedes**. Tú and **vosotros** are used to close friends and to children.

DEMONSTRATIVE PRONOUNS

this one, that one

	m	*f*
this (*one*)	éste	ésta
these	éstos	éstas
that (*one*)	ése	ésa
those	ésos	ésas
that (*one*) over there	aquél	aquélla
those	aquéllos	aquéllas

They agree in number and gender with the nouns they represent.

e.g. **éste** es mi bolígrafo – this is my ball-point.

quiero **esta** postal, **esa**, y **aquélla** – I want this postcard, that one, and that one over there.

The demonstrative adjectives have the same form as the pronouns, except that they are not written with accents.

VERBS

'To be' is translated by **ser** and **estar**.

When it is followed by a noun, or when it indicates an origin, or a permanent or inherent quality, **ser** is used.

e.g. la nieve **es** fría y blanca   snow is cold and white
     soy inglés   I am English
     Inglaterra **es** una isla   England is an island

When it indicates position or a temporary state, **estar** is used.

e.g. el hotel **está** en la calle principal   the hotel is in the main street
     estamos en España   we are in Spain

Present tense of **ser** and **estar**.

	ser	*estar*
I am	soy	estoy
you are	eres	estás
he, she is,	es	está
you are	es	está
we are	somos	estamos
you are	sois	estáis
they, you are	son	están

'To have, to possess' is translated by **tener**.

I have, etc	tengo
	tienes
	tiene
	tenemos
	tenéis
	tienen

e.g. **tengo** mi pasaporte – I have my passport.

'To have' is translated by **haber** only to form compound tenses of other verbs.

e.g. **he** visto el hotel – I've seen the hotel.

I have, etc	he
	has
	ha
	hemos
	habéis
	han

In Spanish there are three types of verbs, distinguished by the endings of the infinitives.

-ar hablar – to speak
-er vender – to sell
-ir vivir – to live

The *present tense* is formed as follows:

hablar	*vender*	*vivir*
hablo	vendo	vivo
hablas	vendes	vives
habla	vende	vive
hablamos	vendemos	vivimos
hablais	vendéis	vivís
hablan	venden	viven

The present tense of some common irregular verbs:

dar, to give	*decir*, to say	*hacer*, to do, make
doy	digo	hago
das	dices	haces
da	dice	hace
damos	decimos	hacemos
dais	decís	hacéis
dan	dicen	hacen

ir, to go	*poder*, can, to be able	*poner*, to put
voy	puedo	pongo
vas	puedes	pones
va	puede	pone
vamos	podemos	ponemos
vais	podéis	ponéis
van	pueden	ponen

querer, to want, to love	*traer*, to bring	*venir*, to come
quiero	traigo	vengo
quieres	traes	vienes
quiere	trae	viene
queremos	traemos	venimos
quieréis	traéis	venís
quieren	traen	vienen

The *past participle* is formed by dropping the infinitive ending and adding the following endings to the stem of the verb.

-ar	hablar – to speak	-ado	hablado – spoken
-er	vender – to sell	-ido	vendido – sold
-ir	vivir – to live	-ido	vivido – lived

Some common irregular past participles:

abierto from abrir – opened
dicho from decir – said
escrito from escribir – written
hecho from hacer – made, done
puesto from poner – put
visto from ver – seen

The *imperfect tense*

	hablar		*vender*
I was speaking,	hablaba	I was selling,	vendía
used to speak,	hablabas	used to sell,	vendías
spoke, etc.	hablaba	sold, etc.	vendía
	hablábamos		vendíamos
	hablabais		vendíais
	hablaban		vendían

Verbs ending in **-ir (vivir)** have the same endings in the imperfect as those in **-er (vender)**.

Irregular imperfect tense of **ser** – to be
era
eras
era
éramos
erais
eran

The *future* is formed by adding the following endings to the infinitives of all regular verbs:

hablar	*vender*	*vivir*
hablaré	venderé	viviré
hablarás	venderás	vivirás
hablará	venderá	vivirá
hablaremos	venderemos	viviremos
hablaréis	venderéis	viviréis
hablarán	venderán	vivirán

THE NEGATIVE

The negative is formed by putting **no** before the verb.

e.g. **no** hablo español – I don't speak Spanish.

VOCABULARY

Various groups of specialized words are given elsewhere in this book and these words are not usually repeated in the vocabulary:

A

a, an	**un, una**	oon, oon-a
abbey	**la abadía**	aba-dee-a
able (to be)	**poder**	po-dair
about	**alrededor de**	al-re-de-dor de
above	**encima (de)**	en-thee-ma
abroad	**al extranjero**	al es-tran-hair-o
accept (to)	**aceptar**	a-thep-tar
accident	**el accidente**	ak-thee-dente
accommodation	**el alojamiento**	al-lo-ha-mee-en-to
account	**la cuenta**	kwen-ta
ache (to)	**doler**	do-lair
acquaintance	**el conocido**	ko-no-thee-do
across	**a través de**	a tra-bes de
act (to)	**actuar**	ak-too-ar
add	**añadir**	anya-deer
address	**la dirección**	dee-rek-thyon
admire (to)	**admirar**	ad-mee-rar
admission	**la admisión/la entrada**	ad-mee-syon/en-trada
adventure	**la aventura**	a-ben-too-ra
advertisement	**el anuncio**	a-noon-thyo
advice	**el consejo**	kon-say-ho
aeroplane	**el avión**	ab-yon
afford (to)	**costear**	kos-tai-ar
afraid (to be)	**tener miedo**	ten-air-myay-do

afraid (to be)	**tener miedo**	ten-air-myay-do
after	**después (de)**	des-**pwes**
afternoon	**la tarde**	tar-de
again	**otra vez**	otra beth
against	**contra**	kon-tra
age	**la edad**	ay-da
agency	**la agencia**	a-**hen**-thee-a
agent	**el agente**	a-**hen**-te
agree (to)	**estar de acuerdo**	es-tar dak-**wair**-do
air	**el aire**	a-ee-re
airbed	**el colchón de aire**	kol-**chon** da-ee-re
air-conditioning	**el aire acondicionado**	a-ee-re a-kon-dee-thyon-ado
alarm clock	**el (reloj) despertador**	(re-loh) des-pair-ta-dor
alcoholic	**alcohólico**	al-ko-lee-ko
alike	**parecido/similar**	pa-re-**thee**-do/see-mee-lar
alive	**vivo**	bee-bo
all	**todo**	to-do
allow (to)	**permitir/dejar**	pair-mee-teer/de-har
all right	**bueno/bien**	bwe-no/bee-en
almost	**casi**	ka-see
alone	**solo**	so-lo
along	**a lo largo**	a lo lar-go
already	**ya**	ya
also	**también**	tam-**byen**

alternative	la alternativa	al-tair-na-tee-ba
although	aunque	a-oon-ke
always	siempre	sy-em-pre
ambulance	la ambulancia	am-boo-lan-thya
America	los Estados Unidos	es-ta-dos oo-nee-dos
American	americano	a-mer-ee-ka-no
among	entre	en-tre
amuse (to)	divertir	dee-bair-teer
amusement park	el parque de atracciones	par-ke de atrak-thyo-nes
amusing	divertido	dee-bair-tee-do
ancient	antiguo/viejo	an-tee-gwo/bee-e-ho
and	y	ee
angry/annoyed	enfadado	en-fa-da-do
animal	el animal	a-nee-mal
anniversary	el aniversario	a-nee-bair-sa-ree-o
annoy (to)	molestar	mo-les-tar
another	otro	ot-ro
answer	la respuesta	res-pwes-ta
answer (to)	contestar	kon-tes-tar
antique	antiguo	an-tee-gwo
any *pron.*	alguno	al-goo-no
any *adj.*	algún	al-goon
anyone/someone	alguien	alg-yen
anything/something	algo	al-go
anyway	de todos modos/ formas	de to-dos mo-dos/for-mas

anyway	**de todos modos/ formas**	de to-dos mo-dos/for-mas
anywhere, somewhere	**en alguna parte**	en al-goo-na par-te
apartment	**el apartamento**	a-par-ta-men-to
apologize (to)	**disculpar**	dees-kool-par
appetite	**el apetito/hambre**	ap-e-tee-to/am-bre
appointment *general*	**la cita**	thee-ta
appointment (to make) *medical, etc.*	**tomar hora**	to-mar o-ra
architect	**el arquitecto**	ar-kee-tek-to
architecture	**la arquitectura**	ar-kee-tek-too-ra
area code	**el prefijo**	pre-fee-ho
argument	**la discusión/riña**	dees-koo-**syon**/ree-nya
arm	**el brazo**	bra-tho
armchair	**el sillón**	see-llyon
army	**el ejército**	e-hair-thee-to
around	**alrededor de**	al-ray-de-dor de
arrange (to)	**arreglar/colocar**	arreg-lar/ko-lo-kar
arrival	**la llegada**	llye-ga-da
arrive (to)	**llegar**	llye-gar
art	**el arte**	ar-te
art gallery	**la galería de arte**	gal-air-**ee**-a dar-te
artificial	**artificial**	ar-tee-fee-thee-al
artist	**el artista**	ar-tees-ta
as	**como**	ko-mo
as much as	**tanto como**	tan-to ko-mo
as soon as	**tan pronto como**	tan pron-to ko-mo

as well, also	**también**	tam-byen
ashtray	**el cenicero**	then-ee-thair-o
ask (to)	**preguntar**	pre-goon-tar
asleep	**dormido**	dor-mee-do
at	**en**	en
at last	**al fin**	al feen
at once	**en seguida/pronto**	en se-gee-da/pron-to
atmosphere	**el ambiente**	am-byen-te
attention	**la atención**	aten-thyon
attractive	**atractivo**	a-trak-tee-bo
auction	**la subasta**	soo-bas-ta
audience	**el auditorio/el público**	ow-dee-tor-ee-o/**poo-blee-ko**
aunt	**la tía**	**tee-a**
Australia	**Australia**	Ows-tral-ya
Australian	**australiano**	ows-tral-ya-no
author	**el autor**	ow-tor
autumn	**el otoño**	o-to-nyo
available	**disponible/listo**	dees-po-nee-ble/lees-to
avalanche	**la avalancha**	a-ba-lan-cha
avenue	**la avenida**	aa-be-nee-da
average	**el promedio**	pro-me-dee-o
avoid (to)	**evitar**	e-bee-tar
awake	**despierto**	des-pyair-to
away	**fuera**	fwair-a
awful	**horrible**	or-ree-ble

B

baby	**el niño**	nee-nyo
baby food	**los potitos**	po-tee-tos
baby sitter	**la niñera/el canguro**	nee-nye-ra/kan-goo-ro
bachelor	**el soltero**	sol-tair-o
back *returned*	**de vuelta**	de bwel-ta
bad	**malo**	ma-lo
bag	**la bolsa**	bol-sa
baggage	**el equipaje**	e-kee-pa-he
baggage cart	**el carrito**	kar-ree-to
bait *fishing*	**el cebo**	thay-bo
balcony	**el balcón**	bal-kon
ball *dance*	**el baile**	ba-ee-le
ball *sport*	**la pelota**	pe-lo-ta
balloon	**el globo**	glo-bo
ballpoint pen	**el bolígrafo**	bol-ee-gra-fo
band *music*	**la orquesta**	or-kes-ta
bank	**el banco**	ban-ko
bank account	**la cuenta bancaria**	kwen-ta ban-ka-ree-a
bare	**desnudo/descubierto**	des-noo-doh/des-koo-byer-to
barn	**el granero**	gra-ne-ro
basket	**la cesta**	thes-ta
bath	**la bañera**	ba-nye-ra
bathe (to)	**bañar**	ban-yar
bath essence	**la colonia de baño**	ko-lo-nee-a de ba-nyo

bathing cap	**el gorro de baño**	gor-ro de ban-yo
bathing costume	**el traje de baño**	tra-he de ban-yo
bathing trunks	**el bañador**	ban-ya-dor
bathroom	**el cuarto de baño**	kwar-to de ban-yo
battery	**la batería**	ba-tair-ee-a
bay	**la bahía**	ba-ee-a
be (to) *permanent/ temporary*	**ser/estar**	sair/es-tar
beach	**la playa**	pla-ya
beard	**la barba**	bar-ba
beautiful	**hermoso**	air-mo-so
because	**porque**	por-ke
become	**hacerse**	a-thair-se
bed	**la cama**	ka-ma
bed and breakfast	**cama y desayuno**	ka-ma ee de-sa-yoo-no
bedroom	**el dormitorio**	dor-mee-tor-yo
before	**antes**	an-tes
begin (to)	**empezar**	em-pe-thar
beginning	**el principio**	preen-thee-pyo
behind	**atrás**	a-tras
believe (to)	**creer**	kray-air
bell	**la campana**	kam-pa-na
belong (to)	**pertenecer**	pair-ten-e-thair
below	**abajo/debajo**	a-ba-ho/de-ba-ho
belt	**el cinturón**	thin-toor-on
bench	**el banquillo**	ban-kee-llyo

bend	**la curva**	koor-ba
berth	**la litera**	lee-tair-a
beside	**cerca de/al lado de**	thair-ka de/al la-do de
best	**lo/la/el mejor**	me-hor
better	**mejor**	me-hor
between	**entre**	en-tre
bicycle	**la bicicleta**	bee-thee-klay-ta
big	**grande**	gran-de
bill	**la factura/el recibo**	fak-too-ra/re-thee-bo
binoculars	**los prismáticos**	prees-ma-tee-kos
bird	**el pájaro**	pa-ha-ro
birthday	**el cumpleaños**	koom-ple-an-yos
bite (to)	**morder**	mor-dair
bitter	**amargo**	a-mar-go
blanket	**la manta**	man-ta
bleed (to)	**sangrar**	san-grar
blind	**ciego**	thee-e-go
blind *window*	**la persiana**	pair-see-a-na
blister	**la herida**	e-ree-da
blond	**rubio**	roo-bee-o
blood	**la sangre**	san-gre
blouse	**la blusa**	bloo-sa
blow	**el golpe**	gol-pe
(on) board	**a bordo de**	a bor-do de
boarding house	**la pensión**	pen-syon
boat	**el barco**	bar-ko

body	el cuerpo	kwair-po
bone	el hueso	way-so
bonfire	la hoguera	o-gair-a
book	el libro	lee-bro
book (to)	reservar	res-air-bar
boot	la bota	bo-ta
border	la frontera	fron-tair-a
bored	aburrido	a-boo-rree-do
borrow (to)	pedir prestado	pe-deer pres-ta-do
both	ambos	am-bos
bother (to) (annoy)	molestar a	mo-les-tar a
bottle	la botella	bo-te-llya
bottle opener	el abrebotellas	abre-bo-te-llyas
bottom	el fondo	fon-do
bowl	el tazón	ta-thon
bow tie	la pajarita	pa-ha-ree-ta
box *container*	la caja	ka-ha
box *theatre*	el palco	pal-ko
box office	la taquilla	ta-kee-llya
boy	el muchacho/niño	moo-cha-cho/nee-nyo
bracelet	la pulsera	pool-sair-a
braces	los tirantes	tee-ran-tes
brain	el cerebro	the-re-bro
branch *tree*	la rama	ra-ma
branch *bank, etc.*	la sucursal	soo-koor-sal
brand	la marca	mar-ka

brassière	**el sujetador**	soo-he-ta-dor
break (to)	**romper**	rom-pair
breakfast	**el desayuno**	des-a-yoo-no
breathe (to)	**respirar**	res-pee-rar
brick	**el ladrillo**	la-dree-llyo
bridge	**el puente**	pwen-te
briefs	**los calzoncillos**	kal-thon-thee-llyos
bright *colour*	**vivo**	bee-bo
bring (to)	**traer**	tra-air
British	**británico**	bree-**tan**-ee-ko
broken	**roto**	ro-to
brooch	**el broche**	bro-che
brother	**el hermano**	air-ma-no
brush	**el cepillo**	the-pee-llyo
brush (to)	**cepillar**	the-pee-llyar
bucket	**el cubo**	koo-bo
buckle	**la hebilla**	e-bee-llya
build (to)	**construir**	kon-stroo-eer
building	**el edificio**	e-dee-fee-thyo
bullfight	**la corrida de toros**	kor-ree-da de to-ros
bullring	**la plaza de toros**	pla-tha de to-ros
buoy	**la boya**	bo-ya
burn (to)	**quemar**	ke-mar
burst (to)	**reventar**	re-ben-tar
bus	**el autobús**	ow-toh-**boos**
bus stop	**la parada**	pa-ra-da

business	**el negocio**	ne-go-thyo
busy	**ocupado**	o-koo-pa-do
but	**pero**	pe-ro
butterfly	**la mariposa**	ma-ree-po-sa
button	**el botón**	bo-ton
buy (to)	**comprar**	kom-prar
by	**por**	por

C

cabin	**el camarote**	ka-ma-ro-te
cable	**el telegrama**	te-le-gra-ma
calculator	**la calculadora**	kal-koo-la-do-ra
calendar	**el calendario**	ka-len-da-ree-o
call (to) *summon/name*	**llamar**	llya-mar
(telephone) call	**la llamada (telefónica)**	llya-mada tele-**fon**-ee-ka
call (to) *visit*	**visitar**	bee-see-tar
call *visit*	**la visita**	bee-see-ta
calm	**tranquilo**	tran-kee-lo
camera	**la máquina fotográfica**	ma-kee-na foto-**gra**-fee-ka
camp (to)	**acampar**	a-kam-par
camp site	**el camping**	kam-peeng
can (to be able)	**poder**	po-dair
can *tin*	**la lata**	la-ta
Canada	**Canadá** *m*	Ka-na-**da**

Canadian	**canadiense**	ka-na-dyen-se
cancel (to)	**anular**	a-noo-lar
candle	**la vela/el cirio**	be-la/thee-ree-o
canoe	**la canoa**	ka-no-a
can opener	**el abre latas**	a-bre la-tas
cap	**la gorra**	gor-ra
capital city	**la capital**	ka-pee-tal
car	**el coche**	ko-che
carafe	**la garrafa**	gar-ra-fa
caretaker	**el portero**	por-te-ro
car park	**el aparcamiento**	a-par-ka-mee-en-to
carpet	**la alfombra**	al-fom-bra
caravan	**el remolque**	re-mol-ke
card	**la tarjeta**	tar-he-ta
(playing) card	**la carta**	kar-ta
care	**el cuidado**	kwee-da-do
careful	**cuidadoso**	kwee-da-do-so
careless	**descuidado**	des-kwee-da-do
carry (to)	**llevar**	llye-bar
cash (to)	**cambiar**	kam-byar
cashier	**el cajero**	ka-hair-o
casino	**el casino**	ka-see-no
cassette	**la casete**	ka-se-te
castle	**el castillo**	kas-tee-llyo
cat	**el gato**	ga-to
catalogue	**el catálogo**	ka-ta-lo-go

catch (to)	**coger**	ko-hair
cathedral	**la catedral**	ka-te-dral
catholic	**católico**	ka-to-lee-ko
cause	**la causa**	kow-sa
cave	**la cueva**	kwe-ba
cement	**el cemento**	the-men-to
central	**central**	then-tral
centre	**el centro**	then-tro
century	**el siglo**	see-glo
ceremony	**la ceremonia**	the-re-mon-ya
certain	**seguro**	se-goo-ro
certainly	**ciertamente**	thyair-ta-mente
chain	**la cadena**	ka-de-na
chair	**la silla**	see-llya
chambermaid	**la camarera**	ka-ma-rair-a
chance	**la ocasión**	o-ka-syon
(small) change	**el cambio**	kam-byo
change (to)	**cambiar**	kam-bee-ar
chapel	**la capilla**	ka-pee-llya
charge	**la tarifa**	ta-ree-fa
charge (to)	**cobrar**	kob-rar
cheap	**barato**	ba-ra-to
check (to)	**examinar**	eg-sam-ee-nar
chef	**el jefe**	he-fe
cheque	**el cheque**	che-ke
chess	**el ajedrez**	a-he-dreth

chess set	**el juego de ajedrez**	hoo-e-go de a-he-dreth
child	**el niño**	nee-nyo
chill (to)	**enfriar**	en-free-ar
china	**la porcelana**	por-the-lana
choice	**la selección**	se-lek-thyon
choose (to)	**elegir**	el-e-heer
Christmas	**la Navidad**	Na-bee-da
church	**la iglesia**	ee-gle-sya
cigar	**el puro**	poo-ro
cigarette	**el pitillo/el cigarrillo**	pee-tee-llyo/thee-gar-ree-llyo
cigarette case	**la pitillera**	pee-tee-llyair-a
cigarette lighter	**el encendedor/el mechero**	en-then-de-dor/me-che-ro
cinema	**el cine**	thee-ne
circle *theatre*	**el anfiteatro**	an-fee-te-atro
circus	**el circo**	theer-ko
city	**la ciudad**	thyoo-da
class	**la clase**	kla-se
clean (to)	**limpiar**	leem-pyar
clean	**limpio**	leem-pyo
cleansing cream	**la crema limpiadora**	kre-ma leem-pee-a-do-ra
clear	**claro**	kla-ro
cliff	**el acantilado**	a-can-tee-la-do
climb	**escalar**	es-ka-lar
cloakroom	**el guardarropa**	gwar-dar-ropa
clock	**el reloj**	re-loh

close (to)	**cerrar**	ther-rar
closed	**cerrado**	ther-ra-do
cloth	**la tela**	te-la
clothes	**los trajes**	tra-hes
cloud	**la nube**	noo-be
coach	**el coche**	ko-che
coast	**la costa**	kos-ta
coat	**el abrigo**	a-bree-go
coathanger	**la percha**	pair-cha
coin	**la moneda**	mo-ne-da
cold	**frío**	free-o
cold cream	**la crema para la cara**	kre-ma para la kara
collar	**el cuello**	kwe-llyo
collect (to)	**recoger**	re-ko-hair
colour	**el color**	ko-lor
colour film	**el carrete de color**	kar-re-te de ko-lor
comb	**el peine**	pe-ee-ne
come (to)	**venir**	be-neer
come in	**¡adelante!**	a-de-lan-te
comfortable	**cómodo**	ko-mo-do
common	**común**	ko-moon
compact disc	**el disco compacto**	dees-ko com-pak-to
company	**la compañía**	kom-pan-yee-a
compartment *train*	**el departamento**	de-par-ta-men-to
compass	**el compás**	kom-pas
compensation	**la compensación**	kom-pen-sa-thyon

complain (to)	quejarse	ke-har-se
complaint	la queja	ka-ha
complete	completo/lleno	kom-ple-to/llye-no
computer	el computador/ ordenador	kom-poo-ta-dor/or-de-na-dor
concert	el concierto	kon-thyair-to
concert hall	la sala de conciertos	sa-la de kon-thee-er-tos
concrete	concreto	kon-kre-to
condition	la condición	kon-dee-thyon
conductor *bus*	el cobrador	ko-bra-dor
conductor *orchestra*	el director de orquesta	dee-rek-tor de or-kes-ta
congratulations	¡felicidades!	fee-lee-thee-da-des
connect (to) *train, etc.*	enlazar	en-la-thar
connection	la conexión	ko-nek-see-on
consul	el cónsul	kon-sool
consulate	el consulado	kon-sool-a-do
contact lens	las lentillas	len-tee-llyas
contain (to)	contener	kon-ten-air
contraceptive	los anticonceptivos	an-tee-kon-thep-tee-bos
contrast	el contraste	kon-tras-te
convenient	conveniente	kon-ben-yen-te
convent	el convento	kon-ben-to
conversation	la conversación	kon-bair-sa-thyon
cook	el cocinero	ko-thee-nair-o
cook (to)	cocer	ko-thair
cool	fresco/frío	fres-ko/free-o

copper	el cobre	ko-bre
copy	la copia	ko-pee-a
cork	el corcho	kor-cho
corkscrew	el sacacorchos	sa-ka-kor-chos
corner	la esquina	es-kee-na
correct	correcto	kor-rek-to
corridor	el pasillo	pa-see-llyo
cosmetics	los cosméticos	kos-me-tee-kos
cost	el precio	pre-thyo
cost (to)	costar	kos-tar
costume jewellery	la bisutería	bee-soo-te-ree-a
cot	la cuna	koo-na
cotton	el algodón	al-go-don
cotton wool	el algodón	al-go-don
couchette	la litera	lee-tair-a
count (to)	contar	kon-tar
country *nation*	el país	pa-ees
countryside	el campo	kam-po
courtyard	el patio	pa-tyo
cousin	el primo	pree-mo
cover	la cubierta	koo-bee-air-ta
crash *collision*	el choque	cho-ke
credit	el crédito	kre-dee-to
credit card	la tarjeta de crédito	tar-he-ta de kre-dee-to
crew	la tripulación	tree-poo-la-thyon
cross	la cruz	krooth

cross (to)	**atravesar**	a-tra-be-sar
cross country skiing	**el ski a campo a través**	es-kee a kampo a tra-bes
crossroads	**el cruce de carreteras**	kroo-the de kar-re-tair-as
crowd	**la multitud**	mool-tee-too
cry (to)	**llorar**	llyo-rar
crystal	**cristal**	krees-tal
cufflinks	**los gemelos**	he-me-los
cup	**la taza**	ta-tha
cupboard	**el armario**	ar-ma-ree-o
cure (to)	**curar**	koo-rar
curious	**curioso**	koo-ree-o-so
curl (to)	**rizar**	ree-thar
current	**la corriente**	kor-ryen-te
curtain	**la cortina**	kor-tee-na
curve	**la curva**	koor-ba
cushion	**el cojín**	ko-heen
customs	**la aduana**	a-dwan-a
customs officer	**el oficial de aduana**	off-ee-thyal da-dwan-a
cut	**la cortadura**	kor-ta-doo-ra
cut (to)	**cortar**	kor-tar
cycle (to)	**ir en bicicleta**	eer en bee-thee-klay-ta
cyclist	**el ciclista**	thee-klees-ta

D

daily	**diario**	dee-aree-o
damaged	**averiado**	a-be-ree-ado
damp	**húmedo**	oo-me-do
dance	**el baile**	ba-ee-le
dance (to)	**bailar**	ba-ee-lar
danger	**el peligro**	pe-lee-gro
dangerous	**peligroso**	pe-lee-gro-so
dark	**oscuro**	os-koo-ro
date	**la fecha**	fe-cha
date *appointment*	**la cita**	thee-ta
daughter	**la hija**	ee-ha
day	**el día**	dee-a
dead	**muerto**	mwair-to
deaf	**sordo**	sor-do
dealer	**el comerciante**	ko-mair-thee-an-te
dear	**caro**	ka-ro
decanter	**la garrafa**	gar-ra-fa
decide (to)	**decidir**	de-thee-deer
deck	**la cubierta**	koo-byair-ta
deckchair	**la hamaca**	a-ma-ka
declare (to)	**declarar**	de-kla-rar
deep	**profundo**	pro-foon-do
delay	**el retraso**	re-tra-so
deliver (to)	**entregar**	en-tre-gar
delivery	**el reparto**	re-par-to

demi-pension	**la media pensión**	me-dee-a pen-**syon**
dentist	**el dentista**	den-**tees**-ta
deodorant	**el desodorante**	de-so-dor-**an**-te
depart (to)	**salir**	sa-**leer**
department	**el departamento**	de-par-ta-**men**-to
department store	**el almacén**	alma-**then**
departure	**la salida**	sa-**lee**-da
dessert	**el postre**	**pos**-tre
detour	**la desviación**	des-bya-**thyon**
develop (to) *film*	**revelar**	re-be-**lar**
dial (to)	**marcar**	mar-**kar**
dialling code	**el prefijo**	pre-**fee**-ho
diamond	**el brillante**	bree-**llyan**-te
dice	**los dados**	**da**-dos
dictionary	**el diccionario**	deek-**thyo**-nar-yo
diet	**la dieta**	dee-**e**-ta
diet (to)	**estar a dieta**	es-**tar** a dee-**e**-ta
different	**diferente**	dee-fair-**en**-te
difficult	**difícil**	dee-**fee**-theel
dine (to)	**cenar**	**the**-nar
dining room	**el comedor**	ko-me-**dor**
dinner	**la cena**	**the**-na
dinner jacket	**el smoking**	es-mo-**keeng**
direct	**directo**	dee-**rek**-to
direction	**la dirección**	dee-rek-**thyon**
dirty	**sucio**	**soo**-thyo

disappointed	**decepcionado**	de-thep-thee-on-a-do
discothèque	**la discoteca**	dees-ko-te-ka
discount	**el descuento**	des-koo-en-to
dish	**el plato**	pla-to
disinfectant	**el desinfectante**	de-seen-fek-tan-te
distance	**la distancia**	dees-tan-thee-a
disturb (to)	**molestar**	mo-les-tar
ditch	**la cuenta**	koo-en-ta
dive (to)	**tirarse de cabeza**	tee-rar-se de ka-be-tha
diving board	**el trampolín**	tram-po-leen
divorced	**divorciado**	dee-bor-thya-do
do (to)	**hacer**	a-thair
dock (to)	**atracar**	atra-kar
doctor	**el médico**	me-dee-ko
dog	**el perro**	per-ro
doll	**la muñeca**	moon-ye-ka
door	**la puerta**	pwair-ta
double	**doble**	do-ble
double bed	**la cama doble**	ka-ma do-ble
double room	**la habitación de matrimonio**	a-bee-ta-thyon de mat-ree-mo-nee-o
down (stairs)	**abajo**	a-ba-ho
dozen	**la docena**	do-the-na
draughty	**aireado/corriente**	a-ee-ra-a-do/kor-ree-en-te
draw (to)	**dibujar**	dee-boo-har
drawer	**el cajón**	ka-hon

drawing	**el dibujo**	dee-boo-ho
dream	**el sueño**	swen-yo
dress	**el vestido**	bes-tee-do
dressing gown	**la bata/el batín**	ba-ta/ba-tin
dressmaker	**la modista**	mo-dees-ta
drink (to)	**beber**	be-bair
drinking water	**el agua potable**	ag-wa po-ta-ble
drive (to)	**conducir**	kon-doo-theer
driver	**el conductor**	kon-dook-tor
driving licence	**el carnet de conducir**	kar-net de kon-doo-theer
drop (to)	**dejar caer**	de-har ka-yer
drunk	**borracho**	bor-ra-cho
dry	**seco**	se-ko
dry (to)	**secar**	se-kar
during	**mientras**	myen-tras
duvet	**el edredón**	e-dre-**don**
dye	**el tinte**	teen-te

E

each	**cada**	ka-da
early	**temprano**	tem-pra-no
earrings	**los pendientes**	pen-dyen-tes
east	**el este**	es-te
Easter	**Pascua**	Pas-koo-a
easy	**fácil**	fa-theel
eat (to)	**comer**	ko-mair

edge	**el borde**	bor-de
EEC	**la Comunidad Económica Europea**	ko-moo-nee-dad e-ko-no-mee-ka e-oo-ro-pe-a
elastic	**el elástico**	e-las-tee-ko
electric light bulb	**la bujía eléctrica**	boo-**hee**-a el-**ek**-tree-ka
electric point	**el enchufe**	en-choo-fe
electricity	**la electricidad**	el-ek-tree-thee-da
elevator	**el ascensor**	as-then-sor
embassy	**la embajada**	em-ba-ha-da
emergency exit	**la salida de emergencia**	sa-lee-da dem-air-hen-thya
empty	**vacío**	ba-**thee**-o
end	**el fin/el final**	feen/fee-nal
engaged *people*	**comprometido**	kom-prom-e-tee-do
engaged *telephone*	**ocupado**	o-koo-pa-do
engine	**el motor/la máquina**	mo-tor/**ma**-kee-na
England	**Inglaterra** *f*	Een-gla-ter-ra
English	**inglés**	een-**gles**
enjoy oneself (to)	**divertirse**	dee-bair-teer-se
enlargement	**la ampliación**	amp-lya-**thyon**
enough	**bastante**	bas-tan-te
enquiries	**información**	en-for-ma-**thyon**
enter (to)	**entrar**	en-trar
entrance	**la entrada**	en-tra-da
entrance fee	**el precio de la entrada**	pre-thyo de la en-tra-da

envelope	**el sobre**	so-bre
equipment	**el equipo**	e-kee-po
escalator	**la escalera automática**	es-ka-lair-a ow-to-ma-tee-ka
escape (to)	**escapar**	es-ka-par
estate agent	**el agente inmobiliario**	a-hen-te een-mo-bee-lee-a-ree-o
Europe	**Europa** *f*	E-oo-ro-pa
even *opp. odd*	**igual**	ee-gwal
even *smooth*	**liso**	lee-so
evening	**la tarde/la noche**	tar-de/no-che
event	**el suceso**	soo-the-so
every	**cada**	ka-da
everybody	**todos**	to-dos
everything	**todo**	to-do
everywhere	**en todas partes**	en to-das par-tes
example	**el ejemplo**	e-hem-plo
excellent	**excelente**	eks-the-len-te
except	**excepto**	eks-thep-to
excess	**el exceso**	eks-the-so
exchange (bureau)	**la oficina de cambio**	of-ee-thee-na de kam-bee-o
exchange rate	**el cambio**	kam-bee-o
excursion	**la excursión**	es-koor-syon
exhibition	**la exposición**	es-po-see-thyon
exit	**la salida**	sa-lee-da
expect (to)	**esperar**	es-pair-ar

expensive	**caro**	ka-ro
express	**urgente**	oor-hen-te
express train	**el rápido**	ra-pee-do
eye	**el ojo**	o-ho
eye shadow	**la sombra de ojos**	som-bra de o-hos

F

fabric	**la tela**	te-la
face	**la cara**	ka-ra
face cloth	**la toalla de aseo**	to-a-llya de a-se-o
face cream	**la crema de la cara**	kre-ma de la ka-ra
fact	**el hecho**	e-cho
factory	**la fábrica**	fab-ree-ka
fade (to)	**decolorar**	de-ko-lor-ar
faint (to)	**desmayarse**	des-ma-yar-se
fair *fête*	**la feria**	fe-ree-a
fair *blond*	**rubio**	roo-byo
fall (to)	**caer**	ka-air
family	**la familia**	fa-mee-lya
far	**lejos**	le-hos
fare	**el billete**	bee-llye-te
farm	**la finca**	feen-ka
farmer	**el agricultor**	a-gree-kool-tor
farmhouse	**la granja**	gran-ha
farther	**más lejos**	mas le-hos
fashion	**la moda**	mo-da

fast	**rápido**	ra-pee-do
fat	**gordo**	gor-do
father	**el padre**	pa-dre
fault	**la culpa**	kool-pa
fear	**el temor/el miedo**	te-mor/mee-e-do
feed (to)	**dar de comer**	dar de ko-mer
feeding bottle	**el biberón**	bee-be-ron
feel (to)	**sentir**	sen-teer
felt-tip pen	**el rotulador**	ro-too-la-dor
female *adj.*	**femenino**	fe-me-nee-no
festival	**la fiesta**	fee-es-ta
fetch (to)	**buscar**	boos-kar
few	**pocos**	po-kos
fiancé(e)	**el novio (la novia)**	no-bee-o(a)
field	**el campo**	kam-po
fight (to)	**luchar**	loo-char
fill (to)	**llenar**	llye-nar
fill in (to)	**llenar**	llye-nar
film *camera*	**el carrete**	kar-re-te
film *cinema*	**la película**	pe-lee-koo-la
find (to)	**encontrar**	en-kon-trar
fine	**la multa**	mool-ta
finish (to)	**acabar**	a-ka-bar
finished	**acabado**	a-ka-ba-do
fire	**el fuego**	fwe-go

fire escape	**la salida de urgencia**	sa-lee-da de oor-hen-thee-a
fire extinguisher	**el extintor**	es-teen-tor
fireworks	**los fuegos artificiales**	foo-e-gos ar-tee-fee-thee-a-les
first	**primero**	pree-mair-o
first aid	**los primeros auxilios**	pree-mair-os ow-see-lyos
fish	**el pescado**	pes-ka-do
fish (to)	**pescar**	pes-kar
fisherman	**el pescador**	pes-ka-dor
fishing tackle	**el aparejo de pescar**	a-pa-re-ho de pes-kar
fit (to)	**sentar**	sen-tar
flag	**la bandera**	ban-dair-a
flat *level*	**llano**	llya-no
flat	**el apartamento**	apar-ta-men-to
flavour	**el sabor/el gusto**	sa-bor/goos-to
flea market	**el rastro**	ras-tro
flight	**el vuelo**	bwe-lo
flint *lighter*	**la piedra**	pye-dra
flippers	**las aletas**	a-le-tas
float (to)	**flotar**	flo-tar
flood	**la inundación**	ee-noon-da-thyon
floor *storey*	**el piso**	pee-so
floor *room*	**el suelo**	swe-lo
floor show	**el espectáculo**	es-pek-ta-koo-lo
flower	**la flor**	flor
fly	**la mosca**	mos-ka

fly (to)	**volar**	bo-lar
fog	**la niebla**	nee-e-bla
fold (to)	**doblar**	dob-lar
follow (to)	**seguir**	se-geer
food	**la comida**	ko-mee-da
foot	**el pie**	pee-ay
football	**el fútbol**	**foot**-bol
footpath	**el camino**	ka-mee-no
for	**por/para**	por/pa-ra
forbid (to)	**prohibir**	pro-ee-beer
foreign	**extranjero**	es-tran-hair-o
forest	**la selva/el bosque**	sel-ba/bos-ke
forget (to)	**olvidar**	ol-bee-dar
fork	**el tenedor**	te-ne-dor
forward	**adelante**	a-de-lan-te
fountain	**la fuente**	fwen-te
fragile	**frágil**	**fra**-heel
free	**libre/gratuito**	lee-bre/gra-too-ee-to
fresh	**fresco**	fres-ko
fresh water	**el agua dulce**	a-gwa dool-the
friend	**el amigo**	amee-go
from	**de/desde**	de/des-de
(in) front	**frente**	fren-te
frontier	**la frontera**	fron-tair-a
frost	**la escarcha**	es-kar-cha
frozen	**congelado**	kon-hel-a-do

frozen (food)	**los congelados**	kon-he-la-dos
fruit	**la fruta**	froo-ta
full	**lleno**	llye-no
full board	**la pensión completa**	pen-syon kom-ple-ta
fun	**la diversión**	dee-bair-**syon**
funny	**cómico/divertido**	ko-mee-ko/dee-bair-tee-do
fur	**la piel**	pee-el
furniture	**los muebles**	mwe-bles

G

gallery	**la galería**	ga-lair-**ee**-a
gamble (to)	**jugar**	hoo-gar
game	**el juego**	hwe-go
garage	**el garaje**	ga-ra-he
garbage	**la basura**	ba-soo-ra
garden	**el jardín**	har-**deen**
gas	**el gas**	gas
gate	**la entrada/la verja**	en-tra-da/bair-ha
gentleman	**el caballero/señor**	ka-ba-llye-ro/sen-yor
genuine	**auténtico**	a-oo-**ten**-tee-ko
get (to)	**obtener**	ob-te-nair
get off (to)	**bajarse**	ba-har-se
get on (to)	**subirse**	soo-beer-se
gift	**el regalo**	re-ga-lo
gift wrap (to)	**envolver**	en-bol-bair

girdle	**la faja**	fa-ha
girl	**la muchacha**	moo-cha-cha
give (to)	**dar**	dar
glad	**contento**	kon-ten-to
glass	**el vaso**	ba-so
glasses	**las gafas**	ga-fas
gloomy	**triste**	trees-te
glorious	**magnífico**	mag-nee-fee-ko
gloves	**los guantes**	gwan-tes
go (to)	**ir**	eer
God	**Dios**	Dyos
gold	**el oro**	o-ro
gold plate	**chapado oro**	cha-pa-do o-ro
golf course	**el campo de golf**	kam-po de golf
good	**bueno**	bwe-no
government	**el gobierno**	go-byair-no
granddaughter	**la nieta**	nye-ta
grandfather	**el abuelo**	abwe-lo
grandmother	**la abuela**	abwe-la
grandson	**el nieto**	nye-to
grass	**la hierba**	yer-ba
grateful	**agradecido**	ag-ra-de-thee-do
gravel	**la grava**	gra-ba
great	**grande**	gran-de
groceries	**comestibles**	ko-mes-tee-bles
ground	**el terreno**	ter-re-no

grow	**crecer**	kre-thair
guarantee	**la garantía**	ga-ran-tee-a
guard	**el guardia**	gwar-dee-a
guest	**el huésped**	wes-ped
guest house	**la casa de hués-pedes/la pensión**	kasa de wes-pe-des/pen-syon
guide	**el guía**	gee-a
guide book	**la guía de**	gee-a
guided tour	**la excursión con guía**	es-koor-syon kon gee-a

H

hail	**el granizo**	gra-nee-tho
hair	**el pelo**	pe-lo
hair brush	**el cepillo de pelo**	the-pee-llyo de pe-lo
hair dryer	**el secador**	se-ka-dor
hairgrips, hairpins	**las horquillas**	or-kee-llyas
hair spray	**la laca del pelo**	la-ka del pe-lo
half	**medio**	me-dee-o
half board	**la media pensión**	me-dee-a pen-syon
half fare	**el medio billete**	me-dee-o bee-llye-te
hammer	**el martillo**	mar-tee-llyo
handbag	**el bolso**	bol-so
handkerchief	**el pañuelo**	pan-ywe-lo
handmade	**hecho a mano**	e-cho a ma-no
hang (to)	**colgar**	kol-gar
hanger	**la percha**	pair-cha

happen (to)	**suceder**	soo-the-dair
happy	**feliz**	fe-leeth
happy birthday	**felicidades**	fe-lee-thee-da-des
harbour	**el puerto**	pwair-to
hard	**duro**	doo-ro
harmful	**dañino**	da-nye-no
harmless	**inofensivo**	ee-no-fen-see-bo
hat	**el sombrero**	som-brair-o
have (to)	**tener**	te-nair
haversack	**la mochila**	mo-chee-la
have to (to)	**deber**	de-bair
he	**él**	el
headphones	**los auriculares**	a-oo-ree-koo-la-res
health	**la salud**	sa-lood
hear (to)	**oír**	o-eer
heart	**el corazón**	ko-ra-**thon**
heat	**el calor**	ka-lor
heating	**la calefacción**	ka-le-fak-**thyon**
heavy	**pesado**	pe-sa-do
hedge	**el seto**	se-to
heel *shoe*	**el tacón**	ta-kon
height	**la altura**	al-too-ra
helicopter	**el helicóptero**	e-lee-**kop**-te-ro
help	**la ayuda**	a-yoo-da
help (to)	**ayudar**	a-yoo-dar
her *adj.*	**su**	soo

hers/his	**suyo/suya**	soo-yo(a)
here	**aquí**	a-kee
high	**alto**	al-to
hike (to)	**ir de excursión**	eer de es-koor-syon
hill	**la colina**	ko-lee-na
hire (to)	**alquilar**	al-kee-lar
his	**su/suyo**	soo/soo-yo
history	**la historia**	ees-to-rya
hitch hike (to)	**hacer auto-stop**	a-thair ow-to-stop
hobby	**el hobby**	ho-bee
hold (to)	**tener**	te-nair
hole	**el agujero**	a-goo-hair-o
holiday	**el día de fiesta**	dee-a de fyes-ta
holidays	**las vacaciones**	ba-ka-thyo-nes
hollow	**hueco/vacío**	we-ko/ba-thee-o
(at) home	**en casa**	en ka-sa
honeymoon	**el viaje de novios**	bee-a-he de no-bee-os
hope	**la esperanza**	es-pair-an-tha
horse	**el caballo**	ka-ba-llyo
horse races	**las carreras de caballos**	kar-rair-as de ka-ba-llyos
horse riding	**el paseo a caballo**	pa-se-o a ka-ba-llyo
hose	**la manguera**	man-ge-ra
hospital	**el hospital**	os-pee-tal
hostel	**la residencia**	re-see-den-thya
hot	**caliente**	kal-yen-te

hot water bottle	**la bolsa (de agua caliente)**	bol-sa
hour	**la hora**	or-a
house	**la casa**	ka-sa
how?	**¿cómo?**	ko-mo
how much/many?	**¿cuánto?/¿cuántos?**	kwan-to(s)
hungry (to be)	**tener hambre**	te-nair am-bre
hunt (to)	**ir de caza**	eer de ka-tha
hurry (to)	**darse prisa**	dar-se pree-sa
hurt (to)	**doler**	do-lair
husband	**el marido**	ma-ree-do

I

I	**yo**	yo
ice	**el hielo**	ee-e-lo
ice cream	**el helado**	e-la-do
ice lolly	**el polo**	po-lo
identify (to)	**identificar a**	ee-den-tee-fee-kar a
if	**si**	see
ill	**enfermo**	en-fair-mo
imagine (to)	**imaginar a**	ee-ma-hee-nar a
immediately	**inmediatamente**	een-me-dya-ta-men-te
immersion heater	**el calentador**	ka-len-ta-dor
important	**importante**	eem-por-tan-te
in	**en**	en
include (to)	**incluir**	een-kloo-eer

included	**incluido**	een-kloo-ee-do
inconvenient	**inconveniente**	een-kon-be-nyen-te
incorrect	**incorrecto**	een-kor-rek-to
independent	**independiente**	een-de-pen-dyen-te
indoors	**interior**	een-tair-ee-or
industry	**la industria**	een-doos-tree-a
inexpensive	**barato**	ba-ra-to
inflammable	**inflamable**	een-fla-ma-ble
inflatable	**hinchable**	een-cha-ble
inflation	**la inflación**	een-fla-**thyon**
information (bureau)	**(la oficina de) la información**	(o-fee-thee-na de) een-for-ma-**thyon**
ink	**la tinta**	teen-ta
inn	**la posada**	po-sa-da
insect	**el insecto**	een-sek-to
insect bite	**la picadura de insecto**	pee-ka-doo-ra deen-sek-to
insect repellent	**la crema anti-insectos**	kre-ma an-tee een-sek-tos
inside	**dentro (de)**	den-tro
instead (of)	**en lugar de**	en loo-gar de
insurance	**el seguro**	se-goo-ro
insure (to)	**asegurar**	a-se-goo-rar
insured	**asegurado**	a-se-goo-ra-do
interest	**el interés**	een-te-**res**
interested	**interesado**	een-tair-es-ado
interesting	**interesante**	een-tair-es-an-te

interpreter	**el intérprete**	een-tair-pre-te
into	**en/dentro (de)**	en/den-tro
introduce (to)	**presentar**	pre-sen-tar
invitation	**la invitación**	een-bee-ta-**thyon**
invite (to)	**invitar**	een-bee-tar
Ireland	**Irlanda** *f*	Eer-lan-da
Irish	**irlandés**	eer-lan-**des**
iron (to)	**planchar**	plan-char
island	**la isla**	ees-la
it	**él/ella**	el/ellya

J

jacket	**la chaqueta**	cha-ke-ta
jar	**el tarro**	tar-ro
jellyfish	**la medusa**	me-doo-sa
jewellery	**las joyas**	hoy-as
Jewish	**judío**	hoo-**dee**-o
job	**el trabajo**	tra-ba-ho
join (to)	**juntar**	hoon-tar
journey	**el viaje**	bya-he
jug	**la jarra**	har-ra
jump (to)	**saltar**	sal-tar
jumper	**el jersey**	hair-say

K

keep (to)	**guardar**	gwar-dar

key	**la llave**	llya-be
kick (to)	**dar una patada**	dar oon-a pa-ta-da
kind	**la clase**	kla-se
king	**el rey**	ray
kiss	**el beso**	be-so
kiss (to)	**besar**	be-sar
kitchen	**la cocina**	ko-thee-na
knickers, briefs	**las bragas**	bra-gas
knife	**el cuchillo**	koo-chee-llyo
knock (to) *door*	**llamar**	llya-mar
know (to) *fact*	**saber**	sa-bair
know (to) *person*	**conocer**	ko-no-thair

L

label	**la etiqueta**	e-tee-ke-ta
lace	**el encaje/la puntilla**	en-ka-he/poon-tee-llya
lady	**la señora**	sen-yor-a
lake	**el lago**	la-go
lamp	**la lámpara**	lam-pa-ra
land	**la tierra**	tyer-ra
landlord/landlady	**el dueño/la dueña**	doo-e-nyo/a
landmark	**la marca/el punto**	mar-ka/poon-to
landscape	**el paisaje**	pa-ee-sa-he
lane	**el camino**	ka-mee-no
language	**el idioma**	ee-dyo-ma
large	**grande**	gran-de

last	**último**	ool-tee-mo
late	**tarde**	tar-de
laugh (to)	**reír**	re-**eer**
launderette	**la lavandería**	la-ban-dair-ee-a
lavatory	**los servicios**	sair-bee-thyos
lavatory paper	**el papel higiénico**	pa-pel ee-hee-e-nee-ko
law	**la ley**	lay
lawn	**el césped**	thes-ped
lawyer	**el abogado**	a-bo-ga-do
lead (to)	**conducir**	kon-doo-theer
leaf	**la hoja**	o-ha
learn (to)	**aprender**	a-pren-dair
leather	**la piel/el cuero**	pyel/kwair-o
leave (to) *abandon*	**dejar**	de-har
leave (to) *go out*	**salir**	sa-leer
left *opp. right*	**izquierdo**	eeth-kyair-do
left luggage	**la consigna**	kon-see-na
lend (to)	**prestar**	pres-tar
length	**el largo**	lar-go
less	**menos**	me-nos
lesson	**la lección**	lek-**thyon**
let (to) *rent*	**alquilar**	al-kee-lar
let (to) *allow*	**dejar**	de-har
letter	**la carta**	kar-ta
library	**la biblioteca**	bee-blyo-te-ka
licence	**el permiso**	pair-mee-so

life	**la vida**	bee-da
lifebelt	**el salvavidas**	sal-ba-bee-das
lifeboat	**la lancha salvavidas**	lan-cha sal-ba-bee-das
lifeguard	**el guardia salvavidas**	gwar-dee-a sal-ba-bee-das
lift	**el ascensor**	as-then-sor
light *colour*	**claro**	kla-ro
light	**la luz**	looth
lighter	**el encendedor**	en-then-de-dor
lighter fuel	**la gasolina**	ga-so-lee-na
lighthouse	**el faro**	fa-ro
lightning	**el relámpago**	re-lam-pa-go
like (to)	**querer**	ke-rer
line	**la línea**	lee-ne-a
linen	**el hilo**	ee-lo
lingerie	**la lencería**	len-thair-ee-a
lipsalve	**la crema de cacao**	kre-ma de ka-ka-o
lipstick	**la barra de labios**	bar-ra de la-byos
liquid *adj.* and *noun*	**líquido**	lee-kee-do
listen	**escuchar**	es-koo-char
little	**poco**	po-ko
live (to)	**vivir**	bee-beer
local	**local**	lo-kal
lock (to)	**cerrar con llave**	ther-rar kon llya-be
long	**largo**	lar-go
look (to)	**mirar**	mee-rar

look (to) *seem*	**parecer**	pa-re-thair
look for (to)	**buscar**	boos-kar
loose	**suelto**	swel-to
lorry	**el camión**	ka-myon
lose (to)	**perder**	pair-diar
lost property office	**la oficina de objetos perdidos**	o-fee-thee-na dob-he-tos pair-dee-dos
(a) lot	**mucho**	moo-cho
loud	**ruidoso**	roo-ee-do-so
love (to)	**querer**	ke-rair
lovely	**hermoso**	air-mo-so
low	**bajo**	ba-ho
lucky	**suerte/afortunado**	soo-air-te/a-for-too-na-do
luggage	**el equipaje**	e-kee-pa-he
(piece of) luggage	**el bulto**	bool-to
lunch	**la comida/el almuerzo**	ko-mee-da/al-mwair-tho

M

mad	**loco**	lo-ko
magazine	**la revista**	re-bees-ta
maid	**la doncella**	don-the-llya
mail	**el correo**	kor-ray-o
main street	**la calle principal**	ka-llye preen-thee-pal
make (to)	**hacer**	a-thair
make love (to)	**hacer el amor**	a-thair el a-mor

make-up	**el maquillaje**	ma-kee-llya-he
male *adj.*	**masculino**	mas-koo-lee-no
man	**el hombre**	om-bre
man-made	**sintético**	seen-te-tee-ko
manage (to)	**arreglárse**	ar-reg-lar-se
manager	**el director**	dee-rek-tor
manicure	**la manicura**	ma-nee-koo-ra
many	**muchos**	moo-chos
map	**el mapa**	ma-pa
marble	**el mármol**	mar-mol
market	**el mercado**	mair-ka-do
married	**casado**	ka-sa-do
marsh	**el pantano**	pan-ta-no
Mass	**la Misa**	Mee-sa
match	**la cerilla**	the-ree-llya
match *sport*	**el partido**	par-tee-do
material	**la tela**	te-la
mattress	**el colchón**	kol-**chon**
maybe	**quizás**	kee-**thas**
meal	**la comida**	ko-mee-da
mean (to)	**significar**	seeg-nee-fee-kar
measurements	**las medidas**	me-dee-das
meet (to)	**encontrar**	en-kon-trar
mend (to)	**reparar/arreglar**	re-par-rar/ar-reg-lar
menstruation	**el período**	pair-**ee**-o-do
menu	**el menú**	me-**noo**

mess	**el desorden**	des-or-den
message	**el recado**	re-ka-do
messenger	**el mensajero**	men-sa-he-ro
metal	**el metal**	me-tal
midday	**mediodía**	me-dee-o-**dee**-a
middle	**el medio**	me-dee-o
middle-aged	**de edad media**	de e-da me-dee-a
middle-class	**la clase media**	cla-se me-dee-a
midnight	**medianoche**	me-dee-a-no-che
mild	**suave**	swa-be
mill	**el molino**	mo-lee-no
mine *pron.*	**mío/mía**	mee-o/mee-a
minute	**el minuto**	mee-noo-to
mirror	**el espejo**	es-pe-ho
Miss	**la señorita**	sen-yor-ee-ta
miss (to) *train, etc.*	**perder**	pair-dair
mistake	**la equivocación**	e-kee-bo-ka-**thyon**
mix (to)	**mezclar**	meth-klar
modern	**moderno**	mo-dair-no
moisturizer	**el humedecedor**	oo-me-de-the-dor
moment	**el momento**	mo-men-to
monastery	**el monasterio**	mo-nas-te-ree-o
money	**el dinero**	dee-nair-o
money order	**el giro postal**	hee-ro po-stal
monk	**el monje**	mon-he
month	**el mes**	mes

monument	**el monumento**	mo-noo-men-to
moon	**la luna**	loo-na
moorland	**el páramo**	pa-ra-mo
moped	**la motocicleta**	mo-to-thee-klay-ta
more	**más**	mas
morning	**la mañana**	ma-nya-na
mortgage	**la hipoteca**	ee-po-te-ka
most	**lo máximo**	ma-see-mo
mosque	**la mezquita**	meth-kee-ta
mosquito	**el mosquito**	mos-kee-to
mother	**la madre**	ma-dre
motor	**el motor**	mo-tor
motor bike	**la moto**	mo-to
motor boat	**la motora**	mo-tor-a
motor racing	**las carreras de coches**	kar-rair-as-de ko-ches
motorway	**la autopista**	ow-to-pees-ta
mountain	**la montaña**	mon-tan-ya
mouse	**el ratón**	ra-ton
mouth	**la boca**	bo-ka
mouthwash	**el enjuague**	en-hoo-a-ge
move (to)	**mudar/cambiar**	moo-dar/kam-byar
Mr	**el señor**	sen-yor
Mrs	**la señora**	sen-yor-a
much	**mucho**	moo-cho
museum	**el museo**	moo-se-o

music	**la música**	moo-see-ka
must (to have to)	**deber**	de-bair
my	**mi**	mee

N

nail	**el clavo**	kla-bo
nail *finger*	**la uña**	oon-ya
nailbrush	**el cepillo de uñas**	the-pee-llyo doon-yas
nailfile	**la lima**	lee-ma
nail polish	**la laca**	la-ka
name	**el nombre**	nom-bre
napkin	**la servilleta**	sair-bee-llye-ta
nappy	**el pañal**	pan-yal
narrow	**estrecho**	es-tre-cho
natural	**natural**	na-too-ral
near	**cerca**	thair-ka
nearly	**casi**	ka-see
necessary	**necesario**	ne-the-sa-ree-o
necklace	**el collar**	ko-llyar
need (to)	**necesitar**	ne-the-see-tar
needle	**la aguja**	ag-oo-ha
nephew	**el sobrino**	so-bree-no
net	**la red**	re
never	**nunca**	noon-ka
new	**nuevo**	nwe-bo
news	**las noticias**	no-tee-thyas

newspaper	**el periódico**	pe-ree-o-dee-ko
New Zealand	**Nueva Zelanda**	Nwe-ba The-lan-da
next	**próximo**	pro-see-mo
nice	**bonito**	bo-nee-to
niece	**la sobrina**	so-bree-na
night	**la noche**	no-che
nightclub	**la sala de fiestas**	sa-la de fyes-tas
nightdress	**el camisón**	ka-mee-soon
nobody	**nadie**	na-dye
noisy	**ruidoso**	roo-ee-do-so
non-alcoholic	**sin alcohol**	seen al-ko-ol
none	**ninguno/nadie**	neen-goo-no/na-dee-a
no one	**ninguno**	neen-goo-no
normal	**normal**	nor-mal
north	**el norte**	nor-te
nosebleed	**la hemorragia nasal**	e-mo-rra-hee-a na-sal
not	**no**	no
note *money*	**el billete**	bee-llye-te
notebook	**el cuaderno de notas**	kwa-dair-no de no-tas
nothing	**nada**	na-da
notice	**el aviso**	a-bee-so
novel	**la novela**	no-be-la
now	**ahora**	a-ora
number	**el número**	noo-mer-o
nylon	**el nylon**	nee-lon

O

obtain (to)	**obtener**	ob-te-nair
occasion	**la ocasión**	o-ka-syon
occupation	**el empleo**	em-ple-o
occupied	**ocupado**	o-koo-pa-do
odd *opp. even*	**desigual**	des-ee-gwal
odd *strange*	**raro**	ra-ro
of	**de**	de
of course	**desde luego**	des-de loo-e-go
offer	**la oferta**	o-fair-ta
offer (to)	**ofrecer**	o-fre-thair
office	**la oficina**	o-fee-thee-na
official *noun*	**el funcionario**	foon-thee-on-ar-ee-o
official *adj.*	**oficial**	off-ee-thee-al
often	**a menudo**	a me-noo-do
oil	**el aceite**	a-thay-te
oily	**grasiento**	gra-syen-to
ointment	**el ungüento/crema**	oon-goo-en-to
OK	**vale**	ba-le
old	**viejo**	bye-ho
olive	**la aceituna**	a-thay-too-na
on	**en/sobre**	en/so-bre
once	**una vez**	oon-a beth
on foot	**a pie**	a pee-e
only	**solamente**	so-la-men-te
on time	**a tiempo/a la hora**	a tee-em-po/a la o-ra

open (to)	**abrir**	a-breer
open	**abierto**	ab-yair-to
open-air	**al aire libre**	al a-ee-re lee-bre
opening	**la abertura**	a-bair-too-ra
opera	**la ópera**	o-pair-a
opportunity	**la oportunidad**	op-or-too-nee-da
opposite	**enfrente (de)**	en-fren-te
optician	**el óptico**	op-tee-ko
or	**o**	o
orchard	**el huerto**	oo-air-to
orchestra	**la orquesta**	or-kes-ta
order (to)	**pedir**	pe-deer
ordinary	**ordinario**	or-dee-na-ryo
other	**otro**	o-tro
our/ours	**nuestro(s)**	nwes-tro
out/outside	**fuera/afuera**	fwe-ra/a-fwe-ra
out of order	**no funciona**	no foon-thyo-na
out of stock	**se ha agotado**	se a a-go-ta-do
over	**sobre**	so-bre
overcoat	**el abrigo**	ab-ree-go
overnight (to stay)	**pasar la noche**	pa-sar la no-che
over there	**por allí**	por a-llyee
owe (to)	**deber**	de-ber
owner	**el propietario**	pro-pye-ta-ryo

P

packet	**el paquete**	pa-ke-te
paddle (to)	**chapotear**	cha-po-te-ar
paddling pool	**el estanque**	es-tan-ke
page	**la página**	pa-hee-na
paid	**pagado**	pa-ga-do
pain	**el dolor**	do-lor
painkiller	**el calmante**	kal-man-te
paint (to)	**pintar**	peen-tar
painting	**la pintura**	peen-too-ra
pair	**el par**	par
palace	**el palacio**	pa-la-thyo
pale	**pálido**	pa-lee-do
paper	**el papel**	pa-pel
parcel	**el paquete**	pa-ke-te
park (to)	**aparcar**	apar-kar
park	**el parque**	par-ke
parking disc	**el disco aparcamiento**	dees-ko a-par ka mee-en-to
parking meter	**el parquímetro**	par-kee-me-tro
parking ticket	**la multa**	mool-ta
parliament	**el parlamento**	par-la-men-to
part	**la parte**	par-te
party	**la fiesta/el guateque**	fee-es-ta/gwa-te-ke
pass (to)	**pasar**	pa-sar
passenger	**el viajero**	bya-hair-o

passport	**el pasaporte**	pa-sa-por-te
past	**el pasado**	pa-sa-do
path	**la senda/el camino**	sen-da/ka-mee-no
patient	**el enfermo**	en-fair-mo
pavement	**la acera**	a-thair-a
pay (to)	**pagar**	pa-gar
payment	**el pago**	pa-go
peace	**la paz**	path
pearl	**la perla**	per-la
pebble	**la piedra**	pyed-ra
pedal	**el pedal**	pe-dal
pedestrian	**el peatón**	pe-a-ton
pedestrian crossing	**el cruce de peatones**	kroo-the de pea-to-nes
pedestrian precinct	**el recinto de peatones**	re-theen-to de pe-a-to-nes
pen	**la pluma**	ploo-ma
pencil	**el lápiz**	la-peeth
penknife	**la navaja**	na-ba-ha
pensioner	**el jubilado/retirado**	hoo-bee-la-do/re-tee-ra-do
people	**la gente**	hen-te
perfect	**perfecto**	per-fek-to
performance	**la representación**	re-pre-sen-ta-thyon
perfume	**el perfume**	pair-foo-me
perhaps	**quizás**	kee-thas
perishable	**perecedero**	pe-re-the-de-ro
permit	**el permiso**	pair-mee-so

permit (to)	**permitir**	pair-mee-teer
per person	**por persona**	por pair-so-na
person	**la persona**	pair-so-na
personal	**personal**	pair-so-nal
petrol	**la gasolina**	ga-so-lee-na
petrol station	**la gasolinera**	ga-so-lee-nai-ra
photograph	**la fotografía**	fo-to-gra-fee-a
photographer	**el fotógrafo**	fo-to-gra-fo
piano	**el piano**	pya-no
pick (to)	**coger**	ko-hair
picnic	**la merienda**	me-ryen-da
picnic (to)	**ir de merienda**	eer de me-ryen-da
piece	**la pieza/el pedazo**	pye-tha/pe-da-tho
pier	**el muelle**	mwe-llye
pillow	**la almohada**	al-mo-ad-a
pin	**el alfiler**	al-fee-lair
(safety) pin	**el imperdible**	eem-pair-dee-ble
pipe	**la pipa**	pee-pa
place	**el sitio**	see-tyo
plan	**el plano**	pla-no
plant	**la planta**	plan-ta
plastic	**el plástico**	plas-tee-ko
plate	**el plato**	pla-to
platform	**el andén**	an-den
play (to)	**jugar**	hoo-gar
play	**la obra de teatro**	ob-ra de te-a-tro

player	**el jugador**	hoo-ga-dor
please	**por favor**	por fa-bor
pleased	**contento**	kon-ten-to
plenty	**bastante**	bas-tan-te
pliers	**los alicates**	a-lee-ka-tes
plimsoll	**la zapatilla de goma**	tha-pa-tee-llya de go-ma
plug *bath*	**el tapón**	ta-**pon**
plug *electrical*	**el enchufe**	en-choo-fe
pocket	**el bolsillo**	bol-see-llyo
point	**la punta**	poon-ta
poisonous	**venenoso**	be-ne-no-so
policeman	**el agente de policía**	ahen-te de po-lee-**thee**-a
police station	**la comisaría**	ko-mee-sa-**ree**-a
political	**político**	po-lee-tee-ko
politician	**el político**	po-lee-tee-ko
politics	**la política**	po-lee-tee-ka
pollution	**polución**	po-loo-**thyon**
pond	**el estanque**	es-tan-ke
poor	**pobre**	po-bre
pope	**el papa**	pa-pa
popular	**popular**	po-poo-lar
porcelain	**la porcelana**	por-the-la-na
port	**el puerto**	pwair-to
porter	**el mozo**	mo-tho
possible	**posible**	po-see-ble
post (to)	**echar al correo**	e-char al kor-ray-o

post box	**el buzón**	boo-**thon**
postcard	**la (tarjeta) postal**	tar-hay-ta pos-tal
postman	**el cartero**	kar-tair-o
post office	**(la oficina de) correos**	kor-ray-os
postpone (to)	**posponer**	pos-po-nair
pound	**la libra**	lee-bra
powder *cosmetic*	**los polvos**	pol-bos
prefer (to)	**preferir**	per-fair-eer
pregnant	**embarazada**	em-ba-ra-tha-da
prepare (to)	**preparar**	pre-pa-rar
present *gift*	**el regalo**	re-ga-lo
president	**el presidente**	pre-see-den-te
press (to)	**planchar**	plan-char
pretty	**bonito**	bo-nee-to
price	**el precio**	pre-thyo
priest	**el cura/padre**	koo-ra/pa-dre
prime minister	**el primer ministro**	pree-mair mee-nees-tro
print (to)	**imprimir**	eem-pree-meer
private	**particular/privado**	par-tee-koo-lar/pree-ba-do
problem	**el problema**	pro-ble-ma
profession	**la profesión**	pro-fe-**syon**
programme	**el programa**	pro-gra-ma
promise	**la promesa**	pro-me-sa
promise (to)	**prometer**	pro-me-tair
prompt	**pronto**	pron-to

Protestant	**protestante**	pro-tes-tan-te
provide (to)	**proveer**	pro-bay-er
public	**público**	poo-blee-ko
public holiday	**el día de fiesta**	dee-a de fee-es-ta
pull (to)	**tirar**	tee-rar
pump	**la bomba**	bom-ba
pure	**puro**	poo-ro
purse	**el monedero**	mo-ne-dair-o
push (to)	**empujar**	em-poo-har
put (to)	**poner**	po-nair
pyjamas	**el pijama**	pee-ha-ma

Q

quality	**la calidad**	ka-lee-dad
quantity	**la cantidad**	kan-tee-dad
quarter	**el cuarto**	kwar-to
queen	**la reina**	re-ee-na
question	**la pregunta**	pre-goon-ta
queue	**la cola**	ko-la
queue (to)	**ponerse a la cola**	po-nair-se a la ko-la
quick	**rápido**	ra-pee-do
quiet	**tranquilo**	tran-kee-lo

R

| race | **la carrera** | kar-re-ra |
| racecourse | **el hipódromo** | ee-po-dro-mo |

radiator	**el radiador**	ra-dee-a-dor
radio	**la radio**	ra-dee-o
railway	**el ferrocarril**	fer-ro-kar-ril
rain	**la lluvia**	llyoo-bee-a
(it is) raining	**llueve**	llyoo-e-be
raincoat	**el impermeable**	eem-pair-me-a-ble
rare *unusual*	**raro**	ra-ro
rash	**la erupción**	e-roop-thyon
raw	**crudo**	kroo-do
razor	**la navaja de afeitar**	na-ba-ha de a-fay-tar
razor blades	**las cuchillas de afeitar**	koo-chee-llyas de a-fay-tar
reach (to)	**alcanzar**	al-kan-thar
read (to)	**leer**	lay-er
ready (to be)	**estar listo**	es-tar lees-to
real	**verdadero**	bair-da-dair-o
really	**verdaderamente**	bair-da-dair-a-men-te
reason	**la razón**	ra-thon
receipt	**el recibo/la factura**	re-thee-bo/fak-too-ra
receive (to)	**recibir**	re-thee-beer
recent	**reciente**	re-thyen-te
recipe	**la receta**	re-the-ta
recognize (to)	**reconocer**	re-kon-o-thair
recommend (to)	**recomendar**	re-ko-men-dar
record	**el disco**	dees-ko
record *sport*	**el record**	re-kord

refill	**el repuesto/recambio**	re-poo-es-to/re-kam-bee-o
refrigerator	**el refrigerador/la nevera**	re-free-hair-a-dor/ne-be-ra
refund (to)	**devolver**	de-bol-bair
register (to)	**certificar**	thair-tee-fee-kar
relatives	**los parientes**	pa-ree-en-tes
religion	**la religión**	re-lee-hee-**on**
remember (to)	**acordarse de**	akor-dar-se de
rent (to)	**alquilar**	al-kee-lar
repair (to)	**arreglar**	ar-reg-lar
repeat (to)	**repetir**	re-pe-teer
reply (to)	**contestar**	kon-tes-tar
reservation	**la reserva**	re-sair-ba
reserve (to)	**reservar**	re-sair-bar
reserved	**reservado**	re-sair-ba-do
restaurant	**el restaurante**	res-tow-ran-te
return (to)	**volver**	bol-bair
return (to) *give back*	**devolver**	de-bol-bair
reward	**la recompensa**	re-kom-pen-sa
ribbon	**la cinta**	theen-ta
rich	**rico**	ree-ko
ride	**el paseo a caballo**	pa-se-o a ka-ba-llyo
ride (to)	**montar a caballo**	mon-tar a ka-ba-llyo
right *opp. wrong*	**correcto**	kor-rek-to
right *opp. left*	**derecho**	de-re-cho
ring	**el anillo/la sortija**	anee-llyo/sor-tee-ha

ripe	**maduro**	ma-doo-ro
rise (to)	**levantar**	le-ban-tar
river	**el río**	**ree-o**
road	**la carretera**	kar-re-te-ra
road map	**el mapa/la guía**	ma-pa/**gee-a**
road sign	**las señales**	se-nya-les
road works	**los trabajos**	tra-ba-hos
rock	**la roca**	ro-ka
roll (to)	**rodar**	ro-dar
rollers *hair*	**los rulos**	roo-los
roof	**el tejado**	te-ha-do
room	**la habitación**	abee-ta-**thyon**
rope	**la soga/la cuerda**	so-ga/kwer-da
rotten	**podrido**	po-dree-do
rough *sea*	**agitado**	a-hee-ta-do
rough *surface*	**áspero**	**as**-pair-o
round	**redondo**	re-don-do
rowing boat	**la barca/el bote**	bar-ka/bo-te
rubber	**la goma**	go-ma
rubbish	**la basura**	ba-soo-ra
rucksack	**la mochila**	mo-chee-la
ruin	**la ruina**	roo-ee-na
rule (to)	**gobernar**	go-bair-nar
run (to)	**correr**	kor-rair

S

sad	**triste**	trees-te
saddle	**el sillín**	see-llyen
safe	**seguro**	se-goo-ro
sail	**la vela**	be-la
sailing boat	**el barco de vela**	bar-ko de be-la
sailor	**el marinero**	ma-ree-nair-o
sale *clearance*	**el saldo/las rebajas**	sal-do/re-ba-has
(for) sale	**se vende**	se ben-de
saleswoman	**la vendedora**	ben-de-do-ra
salesman	**el vendedor**	ben-de-dor
salt water	**el agua salada** *f*	a-gwa sa-la-da
same	**mismo**	mees-mo
sand	**la arena**	a-re-na
sandals	**las sandalias**	san-da-lyas
sanitary towels	**las compresas (higiénicas)**	kom-pre-sas ee-hee-**e**-nee-kas
satisfactory	**satisfactorio**	sa-tees-fak-tor-ee-o
saucer	**el platillo/platito**	pla-tee-llyo/pla-tee-to
save (to)	**salvar**	sal-bar
save (to) *money*	**ahorrar**	a-or-rar
say (to)	**decir**	de-theer
scald (to)	**quemarse**	ke-mar-se
scarf	**la bufanda**	boo-fan-da
scenery	**la vista/el paisaje**	bees-ta/pa-ee-sa-he
scent	**el perfume**	pair-foo-me

school	**la escuela/el colegio**	es-kwe-la/ko-le-hee-o
scissors	**las tijeras**	tee-hair-as
Scotland	**Escocia** *f*	Es-ko-thya
Scottish	**escocés**	es-ko-**thes**
scratch (to)	**arañar**	a-ran-yar
screw	**el tornillo**	tor-nee-llyo
screwdriver	**el destornillador**	des-tor-nee-llya-dor
sculpture	**la escultura**	es-kool-too-ra
sea	**el mar**	mar
seasick	**mareado**	ma-re-a-do
season	**la temporada**	tem-po-ra-da
seat	**el asiento**	a-see-en-to
seat belt	**el cinturón de seguridad**	theen-too-**ron** de se-goo-ree-dad
second	**segundo**	se-goon-do
second hand	**de segunda mano**	se-goon-da ma-no
see (to)	**ver**	bair
seem (to)	**parecer**	pa-re-thair
self-catering hostel	**la hostelería por cuenta propia**	os-te-le-ree-a por kwen-ta pro-pee-a
self-contained	**independiente**	een-de-pen-dee-en-te
sell (to)	**vender**	ben-dair
send (to)	**mandar**	man-dar
separate	**separado**	se-pa-ra-do
serious	**serio**	sair-ee-o
serve (to)	**servir**	sair-beer
service	**el servicio**	sair-bee-thyo

service *Catholic*	el culto	kool-to
service *Protestant*	el servicio	sair-bee-thyo
several	varios	ba-ree-os
sew (to)	coser	ko-sair
shade *colour*	el matiz/el tono	ma-teeth/to-no
shade *sun*	la sombra	som-bra
shallow	poco profundo	po-ko pro-foon-do
shampoo	el champú	cham-**poo**
shape	la forma	for-ma
share (to)	repartir	re-par-teer
sharp	agudo	agoo-do
shave (to)	afeitar	a-fay-tar
shaving brush	la brocha de afeitar	bro-cha de a-fay-tar
shaving cream	la crema de afeitar	kre-ma de a-fay-tar
she	ella	e-llya
sheet	la sábana	sa-ba-na
shelf	el estante	es-tan-te
shell	la concha	kon-cha
shine (to)	brillar	bree-llyar
shingle *beach*	el guijarro	gee-har-ro
ship	el barco	bar-ko
shipping line	la línea marítima	lee-ne-a ma-**ree**-tee-ma
shirt	la camisa	ka-mee-sa
shock	la impresión	eem-pre-**syon**
shoelaces	los cordones de zapatos	kor-do-nes de tha-pa-tos

shoe polish	**el betún**	be-**toon**
shoes	**los zapatos**	tha-pa-tos
shop	**la tienda**	tee-en-da
shopping centre	**el centro comercial**	then-tro ko-mair-thee-al
shore	**la orilla**	o-ree-llya
short	**corto**	kor-to
shorts	**los pantalones cortos**	pan-ta-lo-nes kor-tos
show	**el espectáculo**	es-pek-ta-koo-lo
show (to)	**mostrar/enseñar**	mos-trar/en-se-nyar
shower	**la ducha**	doo-cha
shut (to)	**cerrar**	ther-rar
shut	**cerrado**	ther-ra-do
sick	**enfermo**	en fair-mo
side	**el lado**	la-do
sights	**los lugares interesantes**	loo-gar-es een-tair-es-antes
sign	**el letrero**	le-trair-o
sign (to)	**firmar**	feer-mar
signature	**la firma**	feer-ma
silver	**la plata**	pla-ta
simple	**sencillo**	sen-thee-llyo
since	**desde**	des-de
sing (to)	**cantar**	kan-tar
single	**solo**	so-lo
single room	**la habitación individual**	abee-ta-**thyon** een-dee-bee-doo-al
sister	**la hermana**	air-ma-na

sit, sit down (to)	**sentarse**	sen-tar-se
size	**el tamaño**	ta-ma-nyo
skid (to)	**patinar**	pa-tee-nar
skirt	**la falda**	fal-da
sky	**el cielo**	thee-e-lo
sleep (to)	**dormir**	dor-meer
sleeper	**la cama**	ka-ma
sleeping bag	**el saco de dormir**	sa-ko de dor-meer
sleeve	**la manga**	man-ga
slice	**la porción/el trozo**	por-thyon/tro-tho
slip	**la combinación**	kom-bee-na-thyon
slippers	**las zapatillas**	tha-pa-tee-llyas
slow	**lento**	len-to
small	**pequeño**	pe-ken-yo
smart	**elegante**	ele-gan-te
smell	**el olor**	o-lor
smell (to)	**oler**	o-lair
smile	**sonreír**	son-re-eer
smoke (to)	**fumar**	foo-mar
(no) smoking	**prohibido fumar**	pro-ee-bee-do foo-mar
snack	**el snack/bocadillo**	es-nak/bo-ka dee-llyo
snorkel	**el tubo de respiración bajo agua**	too-bo de res-pee-ra-thyon ba-ho a-gwa
snow	**la nieve**	nye-be
(it is) snowing	**nieva**	nye-ba
so	**así**	a-see

sober	**sobrio**	so-bree-o
soap	**el jabón**	ha-**bon**
soap powder	**el detergente**	de-tair-hen-te
socks	**los calcetines**	kal-the-tee-nes
soft	**suave**	swa-be
sold	**vendido**	ben-dee-do
sold out	**vendido**	ben-dee-do
sole *shoe*	**la suela**	swe-la
solid	**sólido**	so-lee-do
some	**algunos**	al-goo-nos
somebody	**alguien**	alg-yen
somehow	**de alguna manera**	de al-goo-na ma-nair-a
something	**algo**	al-go
sometimes	**algunas veces**	al-goo-nas be-thes
somewhere	**en algún sitio**	en al-**goon** see-tee-o
son	**el hijo**	ee-ho
song	**la canción**	kan-**thyon**
soon	**pronto**	pron-to
sort	**la clase**	kla-se
sound	**el sonido**	so-nee-do
sound and light show	**la actuación audio visual**	ak-too-a-**thyon** a-oo-dee-o bee-soo-al
sour	**agrio**	ag-ree-o
south	**el sur**	soor
souvenir	**el recuerdo**	re-kwer-do
space	**el espacio**	es-pa-thee-o

Spain	**España** *f*	Es-pan-ya
Spanish	**español**	es-pan-yol
spanner	**la llave inglesa**	llya-be een-gle-sa
spare	**sobrante**	so-bran-te
speak (to)	**hablar**	ab-lar
speciality	**la especialidad**	es-pe-thya-lee-dad
spectacles	**las gafas/los lentes**	ga-fas/len-tes
speed	**la velocidad**	be-lo-thee-da
speed limit	**la velocidad limitada**	be-lo-thee-dad lee-mee-ta-da
spend (to)	**gastar**	gas-tar
spice	**la especia**	es-pe-thee-a
spoon	**la cuchara**	koo-cha-ra
spots	**los deportes**	de-por-tes
spot *stain*	**la mancha**	man-cha
spring	**la primavera**	pree-ma-bai-ra
spring *water*	**el manantial**	man-an-tee-al
square	**la plaza**	pla-tha
square *adj.*	**cuadrado**	kwad-ra-do
stage	**el escenario**	es-then-ar-ree-o
stain	**la mancha**	man-cha
stained	**manchado**	man-cha-do
stairs	**la escalera**	es-ka-lair-a
stalls *theatre*	**la butaca**	boo-ta-ka
stamp	**el sello**	se-llyo
stand (to)	**estar de pie**	es-tar de pee-a

star	**la estrella**	es-tre-llya
start (to)	**empezar**	em-pe-thar
station	**la estación**	es-ta-**thyon**
statue	**la estatua**	es-ta-too-a
stay (to)	**quedarse**	ke-dar-se
steward	**el mozo**	mo-tho
stewardess	**la camarera/la azafata**	ka-ma-rair-a/a-tha-fa-ta
stick	**el bastón**	bas-ton
stiff	**rígido**	ree-hee-do
still *not moving*	**quieto**	kee-e-to
still *time*	**todavía**	to-da-**bee**-a
sting	**el aguijón/la picadura**	ag-ee-**hon**/pee-ka-doo-ra
stockings	**las medias**	me-dee-as
stolen	**robado**	ro-ba-do
stone	**la piedra**	pee-e-dra
stool	**el taburete**	ta-boo-re-te
stop (to)	**parar**	pa-rar
store	**la tienda**	tee-en-da
storm	**la tormenta**	tor-men-ta
stove	**el infiernillo**	een-fyair-nee-llyo
straight	**derecho**	de-re-cho
straight on	**todo seguido**	to-do se-gee-do
strange	**extraño**	es-tran-yo
strap	**la correa**	kor-ray-a
stream	**el arroyo**	ar-roy-o

street	**la calle**	ka-llye
street map	**la guía de calles**	**gee**-a de ka-llyes
stretch (to)	**estirar**	es-tee-rar
string	**la cuerda**	koo-air-da
strong	**fuerte**	foo-air-te
student	**el estudiante**	es-too-dyan-te
style	**el estilo**	es-tee-lo
subject	**el tema**	te-ma
suburb	**las afueras**	afwe-ras
subway	**el paso subterráneo**	pa-so soob-tair-**ran**-yo
such	**tal**	tal
suddenly	**de repente**	de re-pen-te
suede	**el ante**	an-te
suggestion	**la sugerencia**	soo-hair-en-thee-as
suit	**el traje (de chaqueta)**	tra-ha
suitcase	**la maleta**	ma-le-ta
summer	**el verano**	bai-ra-no
sun	**el sol**	sol
sunbathe (to)	**tomar el sol**	to-mar el sol
sunburn	**la quemadura de sol**	ke-ma-doo-ra de sol
sunglasses	**las gafas de sol**	ga-fas de sol
sunhat	**el sombrero de sol**	som-brair-o de sol
sunshade	**el toldo**	tol-do
suntan oil	**el aceite para broncear**	a-thay-te pa-ra bron-the-ar
supper	**la cena**	the-na

supplementary charge	**el suplemento**	soo-ple-men-to
sure	**seguro**	se-goo-ro
surfboard	**la tabla de surf**	ta-bla de soorf
surgery	**la clínica**	klee-nee-ka
surgery hours	**las horas de consulta**	o-ras de kon-sool-ta
surprise	**la sorpresa**	sor-pre-sa
surroundings	**los alrededores**	al-re-de-do-res
suspender belt	**el liguero**	lee-gair-o
sweat	**el sudor**	soo-dor
sweater	**el jersey**	hair-say
sweet	**dulce**	dool-the
sweets	**los caramelos**	ka-ra-me-los
swell (to)	**hinchar**	een-char
swim (to)	**nadar**	na-dar
swimming pool	**la piscina**	pees-thee-na
swing	**el columpio**	kol-oom-pee-o
switch *light*	**la llave de la luz/el interruptor**	llya-be de la looth/een-ter-roop-**tor**
swollen	**hinchado**	een-cha-do
synagogue	**la sinagoga**	see-na-go-ga

T

table	**la mesa**	me-sa
tablecloth	**el mantel**	man-tel
tablet	**la pastilla/píldora**	pas-tee-llya/**peel**-do-ra
tailor	**el sastre**	sas-tre

take (to)	**tomar**	to-mar
talk (to)	**hablar**	ab-lar
tall	**alto**	al-to
tampon	**el tampón**	tam-**pon**
tanned	**bronceado**	bron-thee-a-do
tank *reservoir*	**el tanque**	tan-ke
tap	**el grifo**	gree-fo
tapestry	**la tapicería**	ta-pee-thair-**ree**-a
taste	**el gusto**	goos-to
taste (to)	**probar**	pro-bar
tax	**el impuesto (de lujo)**	eem-pwes-to
taxi	**el taxi**	tak-see
taxi rank	**la parada de taxis**	pa-ra-da de tak-see
teach (to)	**enseñar**	en-sen-yar
tear	**la rasgadura/el roto**	ras-ga-doo-ra/ro-to
tear (to)	**rasgar/romper**	ras-gar/rom-pair
telegram	**el telegrama**	tele-grama
telephone (to)	**telefonear**	tele-fo-ne-ar
telephone	**el teléfono**	te-**le**-fo-no
telephone box	**la cabina telefónica**	ka-bee-na tele-fo-nee-ka
telephone call	**la llamada telefónica**	llya-ma-da tele-fo-nee-ka
telephone directory	**el listín de teléfonos**	lees-**teen** de te-**le**-fo-nos
telephone number	**el número de teléfono**	**noo**-mair-o de te-**le**-fo-no
telephone operator	**la telefonista**	tele-fo-nees-ta
television	**la televisión**	tele-bee-**syon**

telex	**el telex**	te-lex
tell (to)	**decir**	de-theer
temperature	**la temperatura**	tem-pair-a-too-ra
temporary	**temporalmente**	tem-por-al-men-te
tennis	**el tenis**	te-nees
tent	**la tienda (de campaña)**	tee-en-da
tent peg	**la estaquilla**	es-ta-kee-llya
tent pole	**el palo de la tienda**	pa-lo de la tyen-da
terrace	**la terraza**	ter-ra-tha
than	**que**	ke
that	**ese**	e-se
theatre	**el teatro**	te-a-tro
their	**su**	soo
then	**entonces**	en-ton-thes
there	**allí**	a-llyee
there is/are	**hay**	eye
thermometer	**el termómetro**	tair-mo-me-tro
these	**estos**	es-tos
they	**ellos**	ellyos
thick	**grueso**	grwe-so
thief	**el ladrón**	la-dron
thin	**fino**	fee-no
thing	**la cosa**	ko-sa
think (to)	**pensar**	pen-sar
thirsty (to be)	**tener sed**	te-nair se

this	**este**	es-te
those	**aquellos**	ake-llyos
thread	**el hilo**	ee-lo
through	**por**	por
throw (to)	**tirar**	tee-rar
thunder(storm)	**la tormenta**	tor-men-ta
ticket *train*	**el billete**	bee-llye-te
ticket *theatre*	**la entrada**	en-tra-da
ticket office	**la taquilla**	ta-kee-llya
tide	**la marea**	ma-re-a
tie	**la corbata**	kor-ba-ta
tight	**ajustado/apretado**	a-hoos-ta-do/a-pre-ta-do
tights	**los leotardos/panty**	leo-tar-dos/pan-tee
time	**el tiempo/la hora**	tyem-po/or-a
timetable	**el horario**	o-ra-ree-o
tin	**la lata**	la-ta
tin opener	**el abrelatas**	a-bre-la-tas
tip	**la propina**	pro-pee-na
tip (to)	**dar propina**	dar pro-pee-na
tired (to be)	**estar cansado**	es-tar kan-sa-do
tissues *paper*	**los pañuelos de papel**	pan-ywe-los de pa-pel
to	**a**	a
tobacco (brown/ virginia)	**el tabaco (negro/ rubio)**	ta-ba-ko (ne-gro/roo-bee-o)
tobacco pouch	**la petaca**	pe-ta-ka
today	**hoy**	oy

together	**juntos**	hoon-tos
toilet	**los servicios**	sair-bee-thyos
toilet paper	**el papel higiénico**	pa-pel ee-hee-e-nee-ko
toll	**el peaje**	pe-a-he
tomorrow	**mañana**	ma-nya-na
tonight	**esta noche**	es-ta no-che
too *also*	**también**	tam-byen
too, too much/many	**demasiado**	de-ma-see-a-do
toothbrush	**el cepillo de dientes**	the-pee-llyo de dyen-tes
toothpaste	**el dentífrico**	den-tee-free-ko
toothpick	**el palillo**	pal-ee-llyo
top	**la cima**	thee-ma
torch	**la linterna**	leen-tair-na
torn	**roto**	ro-to
touch (to)	**tocar**	to-kar
tough	**duro**	doo-ro
tour	**la excursión**	es-koor-syon
tourist	**el turista**	too-rees-ta
tourist office	**la oficina de turismo**	o-fee-thee-na de too-rees-mo
towards	**hacia**	a-thee-a
towel	**la toalla**	to-a-llya
tower	**la torre**	tor-re
town	**la ciudad**	thyoo-da
town hall	**el ayuntamiento**	a-yoon-ta-myen-to
toy	**el juguete**	hoo-ge-te

traffic	el tráfico	tra-fee-ko
traffic jam	el atasco	a-tas-ko
traffic lights	el semáforo	se-ma-fo-ro
trailer	el remolque	re-mol-ke
train	el tren	tren
tram	el tranvía	tran-bee-a
transfer (to)	trasladar	tras-la-dar
transit	tránsito	tran-see-to
translate (to)	traducir	tra-doo-theer
travel (to)	viajar	bee-a-har
travel agent	la agencia de viajes	a-hen-thee-a de bee-a-hes
traveller	el viajero	bee-a-hair-o
travellers' cheque	el cheque de viajero	che-ke de bee-a-hair-o
treat (to)	invitar	een-bee-tar
treatment	el tratamiento	tra-ta-myen-to
tree	el árbol	ar-bol
trip	el viaje	bee-a-he
trouble	la dificultad	dee-fee-kool-tad
trousers	los pantalones	pan-ta-lo-nes
true	verdad	bair-dad
trunk *luggage*	el baúl	ba-ool
trunks *bathing*	el bañador	ban-ya-dor
truth	la verdad	bair-dad
try (to)	intentar	een-ten-tar
try on (to)	probarse	pro-bar-se

tunnel	**el túnel**	too-nel
turn (to)	**dar la vuelta/volver**	dar la bwel-ta/bol-bair
turning	**la vuelta**	bwel-ta
tweezers	**las pinzas**	pin-thas
twin beds	**las camas gemelas**	ka-mas he-me-las
twisted	**torcido**	tor-thee-do
typewriter	**la máquina de escribir**	ma-kee-na de es-kree-beer

U

ugly	**feo**	fe-o
umbrella	**el paraguas**	pa-ra-gwas
(beach) umbrella	**la sombrilla**	som-bree-llya
uncle	**el tío**	tee-o
uncomfortable	**incómodo**	een-ko-mo-do
unconscious	**inconsciente/ desmayado**	een-kons-thee-en-te/ des-ma-ya-do
under(neath)	**debajo (de)**	de-ba-ho
underground	**el metro**	me-tro
underpants	**los calzoncillos**	kal-thon-thee-llyos
understand	**entender**	en-ten-dair
underwater fishing	**la pesca submarina**	pes-ka soob-mar-ee-na
underwear	**la ropa interior**	ro-pa een-ter-yor
university	**la universidad**	oo-nee-bair-see-dad
unpack (to)	**deshacer las maletas**	des-a-thair las ma-le-tas
until	**hasta**	as-ta

unusual	**raro**	ra-ro
up, upstairs	**arriba**	ar-ree-ba
urgent	**urgente**	oor-hen-te
us	**nos**	nos
USA	**Estados Unidos (de América)** *m*	Es-ta-dos Oo-nee-dos (de A-me-ree-ka)
use (to)	**usar**	oo-sar
useful	**útil**	oo-teel
useless	**inútil**	een-oo-teel
usual	**usual**	oo-soo-al

V

vacant	**libre**	lee-bre
vacancies	**hay habitaciones**	eye a-bee-ta-thyo-nes
vacation	**las vacaciones**	ba-ka-thyo-nes
valid	**válido**	ba-lee-do
valley	**el valle**	ba-llye
valuable	**valioso**	bal-lee-o-so
value	**el valor**	ba-lor
vase	**el florero**	flo-rair-o
VAT	**IVA**	ee-ba
vegetable	**las verduras**	bair-doo-ras
vegetarian	**vegetariano**	be-he-ta-rya-no
vein	**la vena**	be-na
velvet	**el terciopelo**	tair-thee-o-pe-lo
ventilation	**la ventilación**	ben-tee-la-thyon

very	**muy**	mwee
very little	**muy poco**	mwee po-ko
very much	**mucho**	moo-cho
vest	**la camiseta**	ka-mee-se-ta
video recorder	**la cámara de video**	ka-ma-ra de bee-deo
view	**la vista/el panorama**	bees-ta/pa-no-ra-ma
villa	**la villa**	bee-llya
village	**el pueblo**	pwe-blo
vineyard	**el viñedo**	bee-nye-do
violin	**el violín**	beeo-leen
visa	**la visa**	bee-sa
visibility	**la visibilidad**	bee-see-bee-lee-dad
visit	**la visita**	bee-see-ta
visit (to)	**visitar**	bee-see-tar
voice	**la voz**	both
voltage	**el voltaje**	bol-ta-he
voucher	**el bono**	bo-no
voyage	**el viaje**	bya-he

W

wait (to)	**esperar**	es-pair-ar
waiter	**el camarero**	ka-ma-rair-o
waiting room	**la sala de espera**	sa-la de es-pair-a
waitress	**la camarera**	ka-ma-rair-a
wake (to)	**despertar**	des-pair-tar
Wales	**Gales** *m*	ga-les

walk	el paseo	pa-se-o
walk (to)	ir a pie/caminar	eer a pee-ay/ka-meen-ar
wall	la pared	pa-red
wall plug	el taco	ta-ko
wallet	el billetero	bee-llye-tair-o
want (to)	querer	ke-rair
wardrobe	el armario	ar-ma-ree-o
warm *food, drink*	caliente	kal-yen-te
warm *weather*	cálido	ka-lee-do
wash (to)	lavar	la-bar
washbasin	el lavabo	la-ba-bo
waste	el desperdicio	des-pair-dee-thyo
waste (to)	desperdiciar	des-pair-dee-thyar
watch	el reloj	re-loh
water (fresh/salt)	el agua *f* (dulce/ salada)	a-gwa (dool-the/sa-la-da)
waterfall	la cascada	kas-ka-da
waterproof	impermeable	eem-pair-me-ab-le
water ski-ing	el esquí acuático	es-kee a-kwa-tee-ko
wave	la ola	o-la
way	el camino	ka-mee-no
we	nosotros	no-so-tros
wear (to)	llevar	llye-bar
weather	el tiempo	tyem-po
weather forecast	el parte metereológico	par-te me-tair-e-o-lo-hee-ko
wedding ring	la alianza	a lee-an-tha

week	la semana	se-ma-na
weigh (to)	pesar	pe-sar
weight	el peso	pe-so
welcome	bienvenido	byen-be-nee-do
well	bien	byen
well (water)	el pozo	po-tho
Welsh	galés	ga-les
west	el oeste	oes-te
wet	húmedo	oo-me-do
what?	¿qué?	ke
wheel	la rueda	rwe-da
wheelchair	la silla de ruedas	see-llya de rwe-das
when?	¿cuándo?	kwan-do
where?	¿dónde?	don-de
which?	¿cuál?	kwal
while	mientras	myen-tras
who?	¿quién?	kyen
whole	todo	toh-do
whose?	¿de quién?	de kyen
why?	¿por qué?	por ke
wide	ancho	an-cho
widow	la viuda	bee-oo-da
widower	el viudo	bee-oo-do
wife	la mujer	moo-hair
wild	salvaje	sal-ba-he
win (to)	ganar	ga-nar

wind	**el viento**	bee-en-to
window	**la ventana**	ben-ta-na
wine merchant	**el vinatero**	bee-na-tair-o
wing	**el ala**	a-la
winter	**el invierno**	een-bee-air-no
winter sports	**los deportes de invierno**	de-por-tes de een-bee-air-no
wire	**el alambre**	al-am-bre
wish (to)	**desear**	de-se-ar
with	**con**	kon
without	**sin**	seen
woman	**la mujer**	moo-hair
wonderful	**maravilloso**	ma-ra-bee-llyo-so
wood	**el bosque**	bos-ke
wool	**la lana**	la-na
word	**la palabra**	pa-la-bra
work	**el trabajo**	tra-ba-ho
work (to)	**trabajar**	tra-ba-har
worry (to)	**preocuparse**	pre-ok-oo-par-se
worse	**peor**	pe-or
worth (to be)	**valer**	ba-lair
wrap	**envolver**	en-bol-bair
write (to)	**escribir**	es-kree-beer
writing paper	**el papel de escribir**	pa-pel de es-kree-beer
wrong	**equivocado**	e-kee-bo-ka-do

X

xerox	**la copiadora**	ko-pee-a-do-ra
X-ray	**la radiografía**	ra-dee-o-gra-fee-a

Y

yacht	**el yate**	ya-te
year	**el año**	an-yo
yesterday	**ayer**	a-yair
yet	**todavía**	to-da-**bee**-a
you	**usted/tú**	oos-te/too
young	**joven**	ho-ben
your	**su**	soo
youth hostel	**el albergue juvenil**	al-bair-ge hoo-be-neel

Z

zip	**la cremallera**	kre-ma-llye-ra
zoo	**el (parque) zoológico/el zoo**	par-ke thoo-o-**lo**-hee-ko/thoo

INDEX